Succulents
Simplified

Succulents Simplified

Growing, Designing, and Crafting
with 100 Easy-Care Varieties

DEBRA LEE BALDWIN

TIMBER PRESS
Portland ❖ London

Frontispiece: Succulents range in size from ground covers to trees that look like something by Dr. Seuss.

Published in 2013 by Timber Press, Inc.

The Haseltine Building
133 S.W. Second Avenue, Suite 450
Portland, Oregon 97204-3527
timberpress.com

Printed in China
Book design by Bree Goodrow

Sixth printing 2017

Library of Congress Cataloging-in-Publication Data

Baldwin, Debra Lee.
    Succulents simplified: growing, designing, and crafting with 100 easy-care varieties/
Debra Lee Baldwin.—1st ed.
        p. cm.
    Includes bibliographical references and index.
    ISBN 978-1-60469-393-5
1. Succulent plants. 2. Succulent plants—Varieties. I. Title.
    SB438.B258 2013
    635.9'525—dc23
                        2012038829

A catalog record for this book is also available from the British Library.

To Sandi, Denise, and Patti

CONTENTS

ACKNOWLEDGMENTS

For their generosity, time, and expertise, I gratefully acknowledge Ken Altman and the staff of Altman Plants, Vista, CA; horticulturist Patrick Anderson; succulent and floral designer Cindy Davison of The Succulent Perch; and Robin Stockwell of Succulent Gardens, Castroville, CA.

For contributing photos, my thanks go to David Cristiani, The Quercus Group, Albuquerque, NM; Marialuisa Kaprielian, Succulently Urban, San Diego; Cristin Bisbee Priest, Simplified Bee, San Francisco; Genevieve Schmidt Landscape Design, Humbolt County, CA; Cate Schotl and Kristi Collyer, Green Thumb Garage, Laguna Niguel, CA; Joe Stead of Orange Coast College, Costa Mesa, CA; David Winger of Plant Select, CO; and Kit Wertz and Casey Schwartz of FlowerDuet, Los Angeles.

Designers, nurseries, artists, horticulturists, and collectors whose skills and creativity enhance these pages include Akana Design; Randy Baldwin, San Marcos Growers; Charles and Debbie Ball; Gary Bartl; Sydney Baumgartner; Jim Bishop; Michael and Joyce Buckner, The Plant Man nursery; Brandon Bullard, Desert Theater; R. C. Cohen; Elisabeth Crouch; Davis Dalbok; Linda Estrin; Laura Eubanks; Robyn Foreman; Good Earth Nursery; Larry Grammer and the Thongthiraj sisters of California Cactus Center nursery; Marylyn Henderson; Don Hunt; Tom Jesch, Waterwise Botanicals nursery; Peter and Margaret Jones; Tony Krock, Terra Sol Garden Center; Randy Laurie; Matthew Maggio; Cara Meyers, DIG Gardens nursery; Patt Miller; Stephanie Mills; Frank Mitzel; Jeff Moore, Solana Succulents nursery; Bill Munkacsy; Susan Munn; Hanh Nguyen; Trang Nguyen, Exquisite Orchids and Succulents; Monika Nochisaki; Oasis Water Efficient Gardens; Frank and Susan Oddo; Jeff Pavlat; Rainbow Gardens nursery; Ravenna Gardens; Roger's Gardens; Mary Rodriguez; Michael and Danielle Romero; Suzy Schaefer; Carolyn and Herb Schaer; Seaside Gardens nursery; Kathy Short and Patti Canoles; Jill Sullivan; Eric Swadell; Rebecca Sweet; Keith Kitoi Taylor; Melissa Teisl and Jon Hawley, Chicweed; Char Vert; Peter Walkowiak; Nick Wilkinson, GROW nursery; and Lila Yee.

Many thanks as well to the Arizona-Sonora Desert Museum; the Cactus and Succulent Society of America; the San Diego Botanic Garden; the San Diego Horticultural Society; Sherman Gardens, Corona del Mar, CA; South Coast Botanic Garden, Palos Verdes, CA; and Tohono Chul Park, Tucson, AZ.

Last but not least, I am grateful for above-and-beyond help from my editor, Lorraine Anderson; from my publisher, Timber Press; and from my beloved husband and tech hound, Jeff Walz.

PREFACE

When people ask me how I became interested in succulents, I tell them I toured an amazing succulent garden on assignment for the *San Diego Union-Tribune*. Horticulturist Patrick Anderson and his aloe garden opened my eyes to the beauty of succulents and their potential in garden design.

Yet even as I say this, around the edges of my awareness floats a much earlier memory. I was eight or nine years old when I went with my mother to a home in a wealthy community for an occasion I don't remember. When we returned home, my mother described the house to my father: "Big picture windows, but imagine having to clean them. Views of the golf course, but the property is too steep. Surrounded by trees, but they shed leaves and bark. Big deck off the living room, but no garden."

No garden? There had been an astonishing one, in pots on the deck, with plants unlike any I'd seen before. They looked like eels, starfish, and coral. One was a perfect little sphere with a green-and-maroon herringbone pattern. Others were necklaces of blue-gray buttons, rubbery silver-blue roses, and sticks of green chalk with windowed tips.

My mother concluded wistfully, "Maybe someday Debbie will have a house like that." Why would I want it, I wondered, if it came with dirty windows, messy trees, and near-vertical land? On the other hand, who wouldn't want that deck garden? It became something I longed for, along with a saltwater aquarium, a hot air balloon, and an unlimited supply of chocolate marshmallows.

I no longer want any of those, but succulents continue to seduce me. I'm that little girl again when I see a succulent I haven't seen before, or even a well-grown one I may have seen dozens of times. You might assume I have a vast collection, and although I do own dozens of varieties, I don't consider myself a collector. Fascination need not be possession. I'm equally happy looking at succulents in a nursery, at a show, or in someone else's garden. In particular, I enjoy capturing and recording succulents' myriad shapes and textures with my camera.

For most of my career, I've written about all sorts of plants. Words are still my first love, but nothing describes a plant or a garden as well as a photo. As I practice this art form, I often think of how "photography" means "writing with light." Camera in hand, I circle a succulent, looking for the best light. In slanted early morning or late afternoon sun, red margins burn neon bright, spines incandesce, fuzzy filaments shimmer, and leaves reveal glowing hues of rose, orange, purple, and blue. As you might imagine, it was difficult to winnow the selection of photos for this book. So many have merit, or illustrate an important point, and I was continually thinking, "But I *have* to show them this one!"

This, my third book about succulents, is a kind of prequel to the previous two. It's a guide for novice enthusiasts, a quick reference for anyone seeking an overview, and a vehicle for presenting design ideas I'm excited about. Throughout, I share my perspective on a subject that has become my passion.

Part One explains succulents' many desirable qualities and suggests how you might use the plants to enhance your garden, regardless of its size. You'll discover how top garden designers use succulents as a three-dimensional palette.

▶ Teaching workshops is an outgrowth of my work as an author of books about succulents. Danielle Moher's newly planted pot contains blue rose echeveria, 'Calico Kitten' and 'Mini Kitty' crassulas, and burro tail sedum.

PREFACE

In addition to what's practical and beautiful, I delve into the bizarre, eye-catching, and collectible. You'll also find out how to keep your succulents looking as good as the day you brought them home from the nursery. These plants survive neglect but when well tended show their gratitude by being even more glorious.

In Part Two, you'll see step by step how to create succulent centerpieces, bouquets, hanging baskets, and more—all fun and useful projects to enhance your home, to celebrate special occasions, and to give as gifts. It's possible to use succulents in ways unthinkable with other plants. Wait 'til you see Laura Eubanks's moss-and-glue method and how Robyn Foreman turns echeverias into long-lasting rose look-alikes. In Part Three, I present my top one hundred plant picks. Most are succulents I've grown myself and would like you to consider, too. All are readily available (or are fast becoming so) and are easy to grow—providing, of course, you understand a few cultivation basics. No worries. No talent is needed, simply an admiration for succulents, an eagerness to learn, and a willingness to experiment.

Above all, I hope to expand your awareness of beauty and increase your desire to use these fleshy, geometric plants to enhance your outdoor living spaces and to express your unique style. Please don't feel intimidated by succulents that are new to you. If you like them, grow them. I'm betting that in no time you'll be giving cuttings to friends.

And now, it is with pleasure that I present my guide (make that *your* guide) to selecting, growing, and designing with these versatile and intriguing plants. May this book serve to enlighten, entertain, and inspire you.

A word about plant names

Although I am a proponent of calling succulents by their Latin names, I've included their common names wherever possible. This makes the plants easier to remember but also may cause misunderstandings. Common names for succulents are not as accurate as their Latin names, and they are not unique to each plant. Bottle palm (*Beaucarnea recurvata*), for example, is not a palm. Several kinds of succulents have a hens-and-chicks growth habit, but only one has the common name hens-and-chicks (*Sempervivum*).

A Latin name is precise. *Echinocereus triglochidiatus* var. *mojavensis* is commonly known as claret cup cactus, but that mouthful of a Latin name accurately describes the plant. *Echino*, from the Greek, means "bristly like a hedgehog." *Cereus* means "waxy," and ceroid cacti are generally columnar. *Tri* means three, and glochids are spines, so *triglochidiatus* refers to spines arranged in clusters of three. *Mojavensis* is an easy one; it means "from the Mojave desert."

I hope you will familiarize yourself with plants' Latin names. In doing so, you'll gain an appreciation of the usefulness of botanical nomenclature and may even come to prefer it.

One

ENJOYING, GROWING, AND DESIGNING WITH SUCCULENTS

Why Succulents are Seductive

IN MY HALF-ACRE GARDEN, I've grown everything from hybrid tea roses to passion flower vines, and nothing has been as trouble free as succulents.

Because these plants-that-drink-responsibly store water in leaves and stems, they won't wilt if you forget to water them, nor will they miss you when you're away. I no longer give a neighbor a key to my house to come and water my potted plants when I go out of town—not since I switched to succulents. I drench them before I leave, move them out of hot sun if need be, and they're fine for at least two weeks.

Succulents start readily from cuttings or offsets, yet the vast majority are noninvasive.

Native to harsh environments, the plants tolerate neglect but flourish when pampered. They're also problem solvers. You may discover, as I have, that succulents do well in challenging parts of your garden where other plants have failed.

Most succulents do need protection from scorching sun in summer and freezing temperatures in winter, and prefer dry environments to those that are rainy or humid. But regardless of where you live, containers enable you to grow and enjoy hundreds of varieties. Nearly all succulents do well in pots, and because containers are portable, it's possible to shelter the plants when the weather turns too hot, cold, or wet.

◀ Offsets that surround the main rosette suggest raindrops on water. Blue rose echeveria (*Echeveria imbricata*) is tough enough to be used in garden beds.

▼ Canary Island aeoniums (*Aeonium canariense*) illustrate the repetitive geometry of many succulents. Those shown here have sun-reddened outer leaves. The plant branches and forms tight clusters of velvety rosettes.

◀◀ The bold leaves of a variegated (striped) century plant in my garden contrast with green aeoniums and orange aloe flowers.

SURREAL SHAPES, TEXTURES, AND PATTERNS

Home gardeners now understand what collectors have known all along: due to their architectural and sculptural shapes, succulents are a joy to behold and a delight to design with. A composition of assorted succulents tends to look good right away. It's hard to go wrong with plants that have simple, clean lines. Geometric succulents—whether in the garden or in pots—provide great definition and are pleasing to look at year-round.

Many succulents (such as echeverias, sempervivums, aeoniums, and graptopetalums) have rosette shapes that resemble flowers. The plants' overlapping leaves suggest fleshy roses, water lilies, camellias, or daisies. But unlike flowers, they don't suffer from the fade factor. Rosette succulents look the same day in and day out—unless they're in bloom, a lovely bonus. And with leaves that come in pastel hues and blues, it's no wonder succulents are being used in bouquets, centerpieces, and corsages. Rosette succulents also look great paired with flowers in

garden beds. And when it comes to creating an eye-catching container display, one large rosette (such as a cabbage-sized ruffled echeveria) often is all you need.

An appealing feature of certain succulents—notably sempervivums and many echeverias—is their hens-and-chicks growth habit. One rosette (the "hen") sends forth smaller rosettes (the "chicks"). With sempervivums, these often are attached to slender, umbilical-cord-like stems. Over time, a hen and its brood, which soon become hens themselves, will fill a pot, window box, or rock garden. To divide or propagate such succulents, cut or wiggle loose one or more offsets and replant.

With so many shapes, sizes, and textures to choose from, you can select succulents that suit your style, your home, and even an event. Rosette succulents are perfect for settings and occasions at which flowers are traditional; prickly succulents hearken to the spare, desert

◀ 'Blue Flame' agave, upper left, and graptoverias, lower right, along with kalanchoes in bloom, 'Blue Glow' agave, columnar *Pachycereus pachycladus*, and silver torch cactus (*Cleistocactus strausii*), provide an arresting combination of shapes and textures.

▲ Chicks of mountain stonecrop (*Sempervivum montanum*, center), have short stems, creating a tight colony. Echeveria and pachyveria rosettes complete the composition.

▼ Colorful sunset aloe (*Aloe dorotheae*) has a symmetrical growth pattern and leaves with rickrack edges.

aesthetic of the Southwest; and agaves and linear succulents (such as sansevierias, and columnar cacti and euphorbias) suit anything sleek and contemporary.

Artists and architects inspired by succulents include Frank Lloyd Wright, who interpreted the saguaro cactus, that icon of the desert Southwest, in a famous abstract stained-glass design. Agaves feature prominently in the landscape of Taliesin West, Wright's winter home and architecture school near Phoenix. One of Georgia O'Keeffe's best-known paintings is of yellow cactus flowers. Mexican artist Diego Rivera, famous for his calla lilies, also depicted cacti and agaves. And during the 1920s, renowned photographer Imogen Cunningham created black-and-white images of agaves, cacti, and aloes that interpret the plants' linear forms via light and shadow.

Edible, herbal, and illegal succulents

Some succulents can be eaten, but most require preparation to be palatable. When consumed raw, some are sour or bitter; others have laxative properties. Two will get you high. One may get you arrested.

ALOE VERA. Despite being widely known and grown, no naturally occurring populations of *Aloe vera* exist. The gel is high in vitamin C and reputed to have numerous health benefits. Its mucilaginous texture and bitter taste are improved when the raw gel is diluted by an equal quantity of water. I slice the leaves lengthwise and use the gel to soothe sunburn, being careful not to get the yellow layer (just under the rind) on my clothes. Not only does it stain; if ingested, it causes cramping and diarrhea.

CACTUS. At my childhood home near San Diego, cactus was a landscape plant favored by my father. It required no irrigation, and installed around the ranch's perimeter formed a thicket that bloomed in spring and served as both firebreak and security fence. Moreover, "When the famine comes, we can eat it," he would say. I didn't realize he wasn't kidding until I saw vendors at an open-air market in Mexico scraping spines off prickly pear cactus pads (nopales) and stacking them for sale. Flowers atop the pads turn into juicy reddish purple fruit that is tasty but filled with indigestible seeds. Both fruit and pads can be eaten raw, but the latter are much better cooked. Also edible:

- **ORGAN PIPE CACTUS** (*Stenocereus thurberi*) has red, golf-ball-sized fruit known as pitahaya dulce.
- **DRAGON FRUIT**, also called pitaya (*Hylocereus*), is a tropical, vining cactus with long, flat, scalloped leaves and brilliant red, pink, or yellow fruits. These are ovoid, with green fins that make them look like midcentury science-fiction spaceships. The flesh is white or red with tiny black crunchy seeds. Though popular in Asian cultures, high in antioxidants, and available in farmers' markets throughout southern California, dragon fruit has yet to become popular here. The texture is grainy

◀ *Aloe vera* is likely native to North Africa, where it has been used as an herb and in cosmetic preparations and lotions since the time of the pharaohs. Supposedly it was integral to Cleopatra's beauty regimen.

▼ Immature, palm-sized opuntia leaves (nopales) are used in salads and egg dishes in Texas and Latin America.

▶ Chalk lettuce, also called mission lettuce, has leaves that are edible when cooked.

and the flavor insipid, but it sure looks pretty sliced on a plate.

- **PERUVIAN APPLE CACTUS** (*Cereus repandus*) has sweet, bright pink fruit. Despite also having the common name pitaya for its fruit, this columnar cactus looks entirely different from vining hylocereus.
- **ORCHID CACTI** (*Epiphyllum* species) are tropical cacti grown mainly for their large, vividly hued flowers. Their bases swell into fruit that is similar to that of hylocereus, only smaller.
- **STRAWBERRY CACTUS** (*Echinocereus*) has red or green fruits that, depending on the species, may be strawberry or raspberry flavored, with hints of vanilla.
- **GARAMBULOS** are the berries of *Myrtillocactus geometrizans*. They taste a little like cranberries but are not as tart.

CHALK LETTUCE. *Dudleya edulis* is a California native that has upright, grayish, powdery leaves shaped like green beans. Raw, they have an unpleasant chalky taste; cooked, they're supposedly much more palatable.

◀ Several species of hoodia can be eaten raw. Though "cactiform," these South African succulents are unrelated to cactus.

▲ A spineless cactus native to southwestern Texas and Mexico, peyote grows in the form of "buttons" that resemble collapsed muffins. These are so bitter that people who ingest them tend to become nauseated and vomit before experiencing any hallucinogenic effects.

HOODIA. *Hoodia gordonii* is a stapeliad, a type of succulent with large flowers that smell like rotting meat in order to attract pollinating flies. Long used by indigenous peoples of South Africa to take away hunger pangs on Kalahari hunting trips, hoodia is reputed to have appetite-suppressant qualities. Because of extreme interest in the plant for this reason, trade is restricted.

PEYOTE. *Lophophora williamsii* has a long history of use in the religious rituals and medicines of Native Americans and can be used legally today by members of the Native American Church. It is a source of the hallucinogenic drug mescaline and is listed by the U.S. Drug Enforcement Agency as a Schedule I controlled substance (high potential for abuse, no currently accepted medical use, safety undefined, can't be prescribed). Because of overharvesting, the state of Texas lists peyote as an endangered species.

TEQUILA AGAVE. *Agave tequilana*, native to Jalisco, Mexico, is important to that country's economy and farmed as a commercial crop. When the agaves are about to bloom, they're cut back so sugars will concentrate in the core, called the *piña* (Spanish for pineapple). This core is harvested in the plant's twelfth year. Liquid extracted from it is fermented and distilled to produce tequila.

YUCCA. Fruit and seeds—as well as flower stems and leaves when young and tender—of banana yucca (*Yucca baccata*) and Mojave yucca (*Yucca schidigera*) can be eaten fresh, or dried and stored. The assumption that yucca roots are edible often arises from confusion with the botanically unrelated yuca, or cassava (*Manihot esculenta*), from which tapioca is made.

▶ The Ruth Bancroft Garden in Walnut Creek, California, sells small tequila agaves in shot glasses.

A RAINBOW OF FOLIAGE

At my potting workshops, I sometimes hold up a light blue pot and ask, "How many plants do you know that are this color?" It seems obvious that none are. Then I show the group a nursery pot full of blue rose echeveria or blue senecio (*Senecio mandraliscae*)—two common succulents that are truly and undeniably blue. I may create a monochromatic arrangement of blue succulents in the blue pot or combine them with succulents from the opposite side of the color wheel, perhaps a red-orange aloe, fire sticks (*Euphorbia tirucalli* 'Sticks on Fire'), or coppertone stonecrop (*Sedum nussbaumerianum*).

In addition to light blue and orange, succulent leaves come in every shade of green as well as varying intensities of yellow, gold, red, crimson, purple, cream, pastels, and combinations thereof. For a surreal landscape vignette or potted garden that looks amazing by moonlight, use several kinds of succulents that have white, silver, gray-blue, or blue-green leaves. For a dramatic yet simple two-plant pairing, juxtapose near-black 'Zwartkop' aeonium with a nonsucculent but comparably low-water bedding plant such as silvery artemisia, red-orange nasturtiums, orange California poppies, yellow coreopsis, or crimson-flowering kangaroo paws.

Because succulents come in nearly every hue, you needn't rely solely on ephemeral flowers for color interest in garden beds, containers, or even in bouquets. Grown en masse, succulents with multicolored foliage make an unforgettable display. Solo, they serve effectively as the centerpieces of potted arrangements or (if large) as garden focal points.

▶ 'Sticks on Fire' euphorbia, blue senecio, red-margined paddle plant (*Kalanchoe luciae*), and a teal-and-lavender caruncled echeveria illustrate the variety of forms and colors found in the leaves of succulents.

◀◀ A seaside garden showcases purple and pink echeverias, 'Sticks on Fire' euphorbias, red sunset aloe, and agaves that stand out yet will stay small and not block the view: artichoke agave (*Agave parryi* var. *truncata*) on the left and tuxedo agave (*Agave americana* 'Mediopicta Alba') on the right.

▲ Many succulents change color depending on growing conditions. At the end of the dry season, leaf tips of drought-stressed *Agave pelona* at Tucson's Arizona-Sonora Desert Museum are red. Rain will turn them green again.

◀ Jeweled aloe (*Aloe distans*) sparkles with tiny amber prickles that line its blue-and-lavender leaves.

▲ 'Joe Hoak' agave is a green so pale it's almost white. The succulent's creamy leaves contrast with a red-painted wall, which repeats the red of the ruffled echeveria in the foreground. Completing the vignette is a swath of blue senecio.

▲ The blue of the pot calls attention to the blue of a pachyveria rosette used as the focal point.

◀ 'Campfire' crassula turns brilliant red when given lots of sun. It's underplanted with chartreuse 'Angelina' stonecrop.

◀ 'Kara's Stripes' fox tail agave (*Agave attenuata*) stands out against a backdrop of blue senecio.

▶▶ In a northern California garden of leucadendrons and evergreens, 'Blue Glow' agave commands the viewer's attention.

BRAKE-SCREECHING BLOOMS

Succulent flowers blaze even brighter than the leaves. Fleshy stems hold moisture, so blooms of aeoniums, echeverias, and kalanchoes (to name a few) are long lasting, on the plant or as cut flowers. In spring, entire hillsides of temperate-climate gardens are blanketed with searing ice plants. Aloes, most of which flower in midwinter, send up spires—often several feet tall—massed with tubular blossoms. And *Kalanchoe blossfeldiana* hybrids, so common they're sold in supermarkets, provide flower clusters in warm hues that range from garish to gorgeous.

When it comes to blooms that are brilliantly colored and undeniably exquisite, the type of succulent that does it best is cactus. Those spiny plants that you swore you'd never have in your garden produce satiny flowers so lovely they'll make your heart sing. Depending on the variety, the bloom show lasts about a week and usually occurs in spring or summer. It's an occasion worth planning your vacation around.

▲ You may hear ice plant before you see it. When in bloom, it hums with bees.

◀ Yellow flowers of near-black 'Zwartkop' aeonium contrast with its dark foliage.

▶ A specimen of *Stenocactus multicostatus* in the collection of Peter Walkowiak blooms in early March.

◀ *Aloe marlothii*, one of the larger aloes, has a branching flower stalk with angular stems lined with orange blooms. This plant is about 6 feet tall (including flowers) and 4 feet in diameter.

Five reasons I like cacti

1. Flowers of many varieties resemble water lilies—a wonderful irony.
2. Some of the most treacherous cacti, like cholla, provide safe havens for birds.
3. The more spines a cactus has, the more beautifully it's haloed when backlit.
4. When their tops or tips are viewed from above, astrophytums and many spherical and columnar cacti resemble snowflakes (another irony).
5. Some—such as Turk's cap, branched saguaros, silver torch cactus (in bloom), and any that are monstrose or crested—are engagingly odd looking.

▲ Few plants bloom more brilliantly than cacti or have such intriguing shapes and spine patterns. This is pincushion cactus (*Mammillaria celsiana*).

▶ In Tucson's Tohono Chul Park, jumping cholla (*Cylindropuntia fulgida*) protects a nesting dove from predators.

◀ A *Pachycereus weberi* tip looks remarkably like a snowflake.

▼ Late afternoon sun makes cacti glow.

▲ Silver torch cactus (*Cleistocactus strausii*) has a sense of humor—or at least doesn't care what people say about it.

BIZARRE AND COLLECTIBLE BEAUTIES

All succulents are intriguing and many are eye catching, but some are so strange they'll make you stop and stare. Eccentric succulents deserve a place of honor in anyone's collection.

Crested growth—which sometimes looks as though the plant's tissues were gathered like fabric along the waistband of a skirt—is a phenomenon found more often in cacti and succulents than in the rest of the plant world. Cresting happens spontaneously, when what would normally be a growth point extends into a line. No two crests are exactly alike. Fasciation—flattening or fanning of stems—is typical of crested succulents and falls under the larger category of monstrose (which includes abnormalities such as points, odd spine formations, twisted leaves, and unusual colors). Such mutant succulents can be rare and valuable, especially when large. Because they sunburn easily and are sensitive to overwatering, crested succulents tend to be challenging to cultivate.

Globular moon cacti (*Gymnocalycium mihanovichii*) are so named because the main plant has smaller "moons" attached. These succulents are also known as hotheads because they come in hot pink, orange, red, yellow, and (more rarely) streaked or mottled combinations. Because these colorful oddities lack chlorophyll, each sits atop—technically, is grafted onto—the dark green stem of a different type of cactus. Give this enough sunlight for photosynthesis but not so much that the grafted top is scorched. Succulents that look like ocean-floor inhabitants include the coral-like crested form of *Euphorbia lactea*; wavy-leaved octopus agave (*Agave vilmoriniana*); Medusa euphorbias with snake-like leaves that radiate from a central point, suggesting sea anemones; and squidlike Van Balen's aloe (*Aloe vanbalenii*), with foliage that makes the plant appear capable of expelling a jet of water and shooting across the garden.

Many succulents also have unusual textures, such as rubbery, velvety, powdery, sandpaper-like, bumpy, webbed, and armed-and-dangerous. Panda plant (*Kalanchoe tomentosa*) has leaves as fuzzy as a teddy bear. 'Sharkskin' agave lives up to its name. Cobweb houseleeks (*Sempervivum arachnoideum*) are covered with white filaments that resemble spiderwebs. Many dwarf aloe cultivars appear encrusted with splinters. Cacti vary from near spineless and pettable to those that will go home with you (not in a good way) if you do more than glance at them. And certain monstrose (convoluted) cacti—such as *Mammillaria elongata* 'Monstrosus'—suggest fuzzy, intertwined snakes.

Arguably the weirdest succulents are echeveria hybrids with randomly caruncled (bubbly looking) leaves. Perhaps because such protrusions resemble lava flows, at least two cultivars have been named after volcanoes: 'Mauna Loa' and 'Etna'. According to echeveria expert Attila Kapitany, all caruncled echeverias are descendants of knobby *Echeveria gibbiflora* 'Carunculata', which has long, narrow, downward-curving leaves.

◄ Octopus agave has tapered, guttered leaves that seem to undulate. In this seaside garden, the plants appear to emerge from rock hiding places.

◀ The only clue that this red pinwheel is a cactus are its spines. Moon cactus is characterized by one or more small spheres that orbit a larger one.

▼ An appreciation for butterfly agave (*Agave potatorum*) isn't difficult to acquire; its cushiony-looking leaves with corkscrew tips are baby-blanket blue. Indentations (bud imprints) form before the leaves unfurl. Whenever I see a toothy agave, I look for such eyelashlike lines.

It's a where's-Waldo effect: which are the stones and which the "living stones"? Pebbles surrounding *Argyroderma patens* mimic the plants' shape and color.

When *Euphorbia lactea* is not crested, the plant—which is columnar—looks nothing like these cream-in-coffee plumes on display at California Cactus Center in Pasadena, CA.

▲ Dwarf Turk's cap (*Melocactus matanzanus*) wears a jeweled crown. Native to maritime Cuba, this tropical cactus likes humidity, warmth, and bright but not searing sun. The fur needs misting several times a week; its purpose is moisture collection.

LOW-WATER PLANTS FOR LAZY GARDENERS

In general, a garden of succulents and comparably drought-tolerant ornamentals needs one- to two-thirds less water than a traditional lawn-and-flowerbed landscape. Less maintenance, too. Typical front yards consist of turf that needs mowing, fertilizing, and dethatching; shrubs that need shaping and deadheading; beds of annuals that have to be replanted seasonally; trees that require pruning; and leaves that need raking.

Envision, instead, a pathway of brick or stone that meanders from sidewalk to front door. Flanking the walkway are berms studded with boulders and agaves, ice plants, yuccas, and an assortment of rosette succulents that resemble flowers. Low-water ornamental grasses that sway in the breeze lend texture and motion. Hummingbirds dart into tubular aloe blooms. Leaning on a wall near the front door is a lawn mower, rusty from disuse, its chassis overflowing with echeverias.

Jade (*Crassula ovata*) is perhaps the most widely grown (and known) of all succulents, doubtless because it is highly forgiving of neglect—something I can attest to. Before I was into gardening, I was given a jade cutting in a shallow pot. It didn't get watered for weeks at a time, only when the leaves became dull and wrinkled. A day or so after being watered, its leaves rehydrated and regained their sheen. Now, more than two decades later, it's still in the same pot, mainly because I'm curious how long it'll last. I suspect the pot will wear out before the plant. It looks much the same as ever, except its trunk is now as thick as my arm. Typical of jade, it prunes itself—limbs shrivel and drop off, seeking soil in which to root. With no help from me, it has turned itself into a balanced bonsai.

PART ONE: ENJOYING, GROWING, AND DESIGNING WITH SUCCULENTS

► If you live where rainfall is sparse, humidity is low, and temperatures seldom go below 30 or above 100 degrees F, here's a colorful, easy-care, water-wise, low-maintenance combination of succulents: chartreuse 'Angelina' sedum, blue rose echeveria, red paddle plants, golden barrel cactus (*Echinocactus grusonii*), and 'Crosby's Prolific' aloe (in bloom). This last earned its name for offsetting freely and flowering abundantly.

◄◄ With no water except dew for three months, these graptopetalum rosettes have shut down to conserve their resources. They've not grown since the soil dried, and they show wrinkling at the leaf tips. Inner leaves have folded around each rosette's core to protect it from desiccation. Yet these would make viable cuttings and when watered will become plump again.

▲ Leaves of a graptopetalum that receives regular water are plump and blue.

▲ Succulents of varying heights and sizes enhance a front yard. Rocks ranging from pebbles to boulders echo similar stones in the home's architecture.

◀ As illustrated by a sliced-open leaf of *Aloe vera*, the defining characteristic of succulents is their ability to store moisture. The fleshier the succulent (cacti and certain euphorbias being among the fattest), the longer a succulent can—and should—go between waterings.

◀ In a drought-tolerant, easy-care landscape for an arid climate, silver Huachuca agave (*Agave parryi* var. *huachucensis*) combines well with columnar cacti and a tree aloe.

▶ Because it's basically a water tank, a golden barrel cactus much larger than a basketball may be too heavy to lift. When transplanting a cactus, do as my neighbor Elisabeth Crouch does: wear thick leather gardening gloves and cushion the plant with crumpled newspaper.

◀ Fine-leaved succulents, such as English stonecrop (*Sedum anglicum*) and dainty *Crassula pubescens*, store less water than their chubbier cousins and therefore need more frequent watering.

Good riddance to your lawn

A lawn requires more water per square foot than anything else you might grow in the same space. It's an ideal play surface for children, but for most activities, 500 to 800 square feet is plenty. Ground-cover succulents are one alternative to replace sections of lawn that do not need to serve as a play space or take foot traffic. Succulents need infrequent maintenance (about four times a year) and when established keep weeds at bay.

Blue senecio starts readily from cuttings and grows 6 to 8 inches high. The leaves—which resemble French fries—are bright blue. It does well on slopes and is lovely planted in drifts. New growth is at the tips of ever-lengthening stems. The best time to trim these back is early fall, when the plant emerges from summer dormancy. Pruned stems will branch, creating more compact plants. Cuttings can be used to fill gaps or to extend existing plantings.

If you're old enough—and observant enough—you may recall that red apple (*Aptenia cordifolia*) was uncommon in southern and coastal California prior to the sixties. Once introduced, it became the go-to ground cover for homeowners who preferred not to spend time gardening. Unlike lampranthus and drosanthemum ice plants that root as they spread, red apple has a single taproot, which makes it vulnerable to gophers. Other than that, red apple is convenient, inexpensive, trouble free, and drought tolerant. Variegated red apple (*Aptenia cordifolia* 'Variegata') is green-and-cream striped. If you live in a colder climate, consider a delosperma ice plant that blooms brilliantly in spring.

Unfortunately, in some areas, "ice plant" has become synonymous with one of the few invasive succulents: *Carpobrotus edulis*, sometimes called pickleweed or Hottentot fig. For decades, it has been planted extensively throughout California to cover slopes alongside highways, which the plant does admirably. Carpobrotus can get by on rainfall alone, is green year-round (red when stressed by drought), has yellow or pink flowers, and effectively chokes out weeds. However, it has naturalized in many areas, including along the coast, where its weight may destabilize cliffs and its unchecked growth prevents native plants from gaining a toehold. If you really want it, carpobrotus grows effortlessly from cuttings. Just don't let it escape your yard.

No succulent ground cover can be trod upon, but drought-tolerant dymondia is a perennial that can be, once established. Dymondia forms a tight mat of slender green leaves with white undersides. It needs slightly more water than ice plant, plus protection from harsh sun.

▶ Blue senecio is a truly blue ground cover. Here it's accented with graptopetalums (in bloom) and aloes in the background.

▼ Red apple ice plant, so named for its red flowers, is a common ground cover in frost-free areas; this is its seldom-seen variegate.

▲ Is there such a thing as a hot ice plant? The *Delosperma* cultivar bearing the trade name Fire Spinner, introduced in 2012, is a vigorous, 4-inch-high ground cover that produces orange-and-magenta flowers for three months, then sporadically the rest of the year. Shown here in the Denver Botanic Garden, it originated in South Africa, where it grows at an elevation of 6,000 feet.

TOUGH PLANTS FOR PROBLEM AREAS

In their native habitats, succulents routinely endure adverse conditions. Most have thick skins—literally—and remarkable regenerative capabilities. They may etiolate (stretch) if given too little light, have beige patches if given too much, be home to mealybugs if air circulation is minimal, and even become severed from their roots—and yet they survive. Not surprisingly, succulents may be the answer for parts of your yard where no other plants will grow.

One such area is the "hell strip" (so named because of the gardening challenges it presents) between sidewalk and curb. This narrow piece of land may have no irrigation, have hard-packed soil, and be subject to foot traffic and dogs. One designer tackled this by mounding the soil and adding boulders, while reserving a flat space that enables passengers to exit parked cars. Next, he installed succulents that over time won't encroach on the sidewalk or street, or poke passersby with spines or pointed tips. A topdressing of pea gravel adds a finishing touch.

Narrow side yards, balconies, and window boxes—often too shady or blazing hot and difficult to irrigate—are garden challenges. Plants in such locations need to thrive on neglect, stay compact, and look good over the long term. Not only do succulents meet these criteria, but they also benefit from a characteristic of tight spaces close to structures: warmth. It's possible to grow succulents up against a house when cold temperatures out in the open might be harmful.

PART ONE: ENJOYING, GROWING, AND DESIGNING WITH SUCCULENTS

▶ A long, narrow flower bed that receives minimal water is within steps of beach and bay. Succulents chosen to suggest undersea flora include sansevierias, echeverias, and small aloes.

Sun-loving succulents for such situations include small aloes, jade and other crassulas, columnar euphorbias, 'Angelina' sedum, blue senecio, and variegated elephant's food (*Portulacaria afra* 'Variegata'). Shade lovers include sansevierias, fairy crassula (*Crassula multicava*), supermarket kalanchoe (*Kalanchoe blossfeldiana*), golden Japanese sedum (*Sedum makinoi* 'Ogon'), light-colored echeverias, and 'Sunburst' aeonium.

Additional challenging situations include those in which a window faces a wall or fence, or when an outdoor living area needs greenery but is too small for the inclusion of even a flowerpot. One answer is a vertical garden. Among the

◀◀ A curb strip planted with aloes, agaves, and jade needs minimal water and is low maintenance.

◀ Fairy crassula, one of the few shade succulents for the garden, is so common in California, it's seldom sold in nurseries; you may have to ask a neighbor for cuttings. I grow it on a slope beneath a deck and trees, and it chokes out weeds and is green year-round. Fairy crassula also conceals fallen leaves, which disappear into it. The downsides of this relative of the jade plant are that it can get too happy if given regular water and rich soil, is not particularly interesting to look at, and is too rangy for container gardens. The name may have to do with airy flower spikes of dainty white stars.

◀ Blue and pink echeverias grow in a soil-filled cloth tube attached to a trellis—a simple but effective vertical garden.

▼ Torch aloe, so named for the shape and color of the flower spikes, is widely grown throughout coastal and southern California. These healthy specimens are seen in the San Diego Wild Animal Park.

▶▶ In 2007, torch aloe helped to protect a home in Rancho Santa Fe during a wildfire that destroyed nearby houses.

many trailing succulents that work well for this are wax flower (*Hoya carnosa*), string of pearls (*Senecio rowleyanus*), rosary vine (*Ceropegia woodii*), burro tail (*Sedum burrito*), and tropical cacti (hatiora, rhipsalis, and schlumbergera).

Steep slopes also present gardening challenges. For a full-sun slope, ice plants are a good solution; they will grow in nutrient-poor, rocky soil and can help prevent erosion by diffusing the impact of rain. In such situations, those that root as they spread (such as drosanthemum, delosperma, or lampranthus) are best because they knit the soil together. For shade, fairy crassula (*Crassula multicava*) can't be beat. It spreads effortlessly without being invasive and has bright green leaves the size of silver dollars. It's frost tender, but once established, it will lose only its top growth and emerging flower spikes in a cold snap. In spring, new growth will hide frost-burned leaves. And frost may not be a concern at all if fairy crassula grows beneath trees, which provide a microclimate (that is, a distinct set of growing conditions in a small area) that is several degrees warmer than the open garden.

If you live in a backcountry area where succulents thrive outdoors year-round, consider the plants a weapon in your arsenal against brush fires. In the intense heat of a wildfire, even gel-filled aloes blacken and turn to ash, but unlike many trees, shrubs, and grasses, succulents are slow to catch on fire and don't transmit flames. Nor does the plants' foliage contain flammable oils or other volatile chemicals. Common succulents that thrive in dry, sunny areas typical of fire-prone sites, and that are useful as firebreak plants, include jade, prickly pear cactus (*Opuntia ficus-indica*), century plant (*Agave americana*), and Mexican fence post (*Pachycereus marginatus*); and the ironically named fire sticks (*Euphorbia tirucalli* 'Sticks on Fire') and torch

aloe (*Aloe arborescens*). Less common is *Aloe ciliaris* 'Firewall', a plant introduced by Tom Jesch of Waterwise Botanicals nursery in Escondido, CA; it forms a low-growing ornamental hedge proven to extinguish flames.

Yet another problem-solving use for succulents has to do with their keep-away qualities. I once asked a succulent enthusiast if agaves beneath one of her home's windows didn't make it difficult to clean the glass. She replied that any inconvenience was worth it. Her neighborhood had experienced break-ins, and she was concerned a thief would attempt to enter her house through its most vulnerable access point—that particular window. In addition to enhancing her garden's appearance, the agaves' toothed leaves and long terminal spines provided peace of mind.

Keeping
Your
Succulents
Fat and Sassy

CERTAIN SUCCULENTS HAVE long been used in coastal and southern California landscapes because the plants require almost no water or upkeep. My parents' home northeast of San Diego had a large garden, much of which had to be hand-watered. A timer would *ding* and my father would stop whatever he was doing to reposition one or more sprinklers. He didn't take this lightly; dozens of edible and ornamental plants would be imperiled if, during a late-summer heat wave, a daily watering was missed. Those plants that would survive regardless were indigenous, succulent, or both.

Jades, aloes, yuccas, agaves, and cacti were, to my father's way of thinking, the best sort of plants: low maintenance, low water, green year-round, and free if a friend or neighbor would provide cuttings. Years later, when my husband and I bought our home, much of the backyard was bare dirt. We had no budget for plants, but it didn't matter; I knew where to go for freebies. My father helped me plant cuttings of succulents gleaned from his garden, but I didn't view them as special. While I busied myself with more challenging ornamentals—such as roses, bulbs, and tropicals—jade, torch aloe, and fairy crassula grew in decomposed granite, oak leaf duff, and dappled shade, spreading slowly but looking much the same year after year.

It is with relief that I've come full circle, embracing the plants of my childhood (except prickly pear cactus, ha). It's hard to generalize about plants so varied, even though all have in common water-storage abilities. Whenever I encounter a succulent I'm unfamiliar with, I experience interest mingled with trepidation. It could be finicky. The first thing I want to know is: Where is its native habitat? Some are from the desert Southwest; others, Madagascar, South Africa, Europe, or the rain forests of Brazil. My garden, and doubtless yours as well, has similarities to those locales as well as significant differences. The key is to utilize the former and compensate for the latter.

This chapter is a primer on what to do after you bring a succulent home from the nursery or receive a cutting from someone. Included is information on climate, light, overwintering, and watering; potting mixes; and how to recognize and eliminate pests. I also go into propagation, in the hope of inspiring you to become a veritable Johnny Appleseed of succulents—someone who will pass along fascinating, low-maintenance, and water-wise plants to family members and friends.

PROTECTION FROM FROST AND SCORCHING SUN

Apart from sedums and sempervivums (and a few other genera, but those are the main ones), succulents come from warm, arid climates. Although the majority can tolerate temperatures down to freezing (32 degrees F) and in excess of 100 degrees F (if shaded), between 45 and 85 degrees F is ideal. During periods of frost or extreme heat, most succulents grown outdoors need to be protected beneath latticework, shade cloth, or lacy trees.

It's an unfortunate misconception that all succulents prefer desert conditions. True, most succulents when actively growing (generally, in spring and summer) like a lot of light, and very few thrive in full shade. However, succulents—especially when small—need protection from harsh sun, especially when temperatures exceed 90 degrees F. In general, those with solid green or pale, variegated foliage are most in danger of sunburn; those that are red, gray, blue, brown, or densely spined are better equipped to handle the sun's rays.

As for indoor plants, if your home's windows aren't UV-treated, take care not to place any plant too close to the panes, lest the sun's rays, intensified by the glass, burn the leaves. If it's not possible to move your succulents a safe distance and still provide the brightness they need, a sheer curtain can be the perfect solution.

In my garden, which is in the foothills of San Diego County at an elevation of 1,500 feet, temperatures typically range from the high 20s F in January to 105 degrees F in August. Being inland, my garden lacks coastal San Diego's ideal maritime climate for succulents, yet I grow nearly every plant shown in this book and the two that preceded it. I situate succulents in three microclimates that moderate temperatures: the dappled shade of trees; near my home's hardscape or walls; and at the top of the slope, because cold winter air, being heavier than warm, flows downhill.

When in doubt, grow succulents in pots that can be covered or relocated as needed. Hundreds of different kinds of succulents do well in containers, and even those with the potential to become immense will naturally dwarf in a pot. Just as a fish will not grow too large for its aquarium, so many succulents will stay small when confined in a container. Once planted in the garden where their roots can spread, those same succulents eventually attain their full size.

If you live where winter means frequent rainstorms and freezing temperatures, shelter your container-grown succulents whenever the weather turns cold and wet. During the plants' winter rest (dormancy), keep them below 60 degrees F, because many need cool winter temperatures in order to flower in spring. (Summer-dormant winter growers, such as aeoniums and senecios, should be overwintered in your home's warmer areas.) Succulents need ten to twelve hours of light daily in winter, but this needn't be broad-spectrum—fluorescent is fine, and economical. One option is to situate the plants in a basement beneath 40-watt (or equivalent, if fluorescent) bulbs on timers. Provide good air circulation to keep pests at bay, and water lightly and minimally—once a month is plenty. Don't water rotund cacti, euphorbias, or living stones at all. As succulents awaken and show new growth, apply a balanced liquid fertilizer diluted half-and-half with water. One feeding a year is adequate, although commercial growers fertilize more often to promote lush, rapid growth.

▲ Queen Victoria agave (*Agave victoriae-reginae*) is a fairly common cold-tolerant succulent (to 10 degrees F) that gets about a foot in diameter.

◀◀ In a Colorado rock garden at 8,000 feet elevation, these stonecrops survive year-round. The plants die back in winter and return in spring.

As soon as the weather turns dependably dry and warm, reintroduce your succulents to sunshine gradually lest they burn.

As for succulents in the open garden, what they tolerate may surprise you. What doesn't kill them can make them tougher. The practice of not coddling plants is called "growing them hard," as opposed to similar plants "grown soft" in the ideal environment of a greenhouse or nursery. This is the origin of the term "hardened off," meaning to gradually acclimate a plant to a harsher environment. In some cases, the leaves actually do become harder, which makes them more pest and disease resistant.

Pay attention to where a new succulent was located at the nursery—whether in full sun, part shade, or a greenhouse—and replicate that, at least at first. If it was coddled but is a good plant for the open garden, introduce it to its final destination incrementally, giving it a half an hour of additional exposure to colder temperatures or harsher sunlight each day. I sometimes shelter newly planted succulents beneath a makeshift tent of old window screens or leafy branches trimmed from trees, or I simply place a patio chair over the plants.

Keep in mind how the sun moves throughout the day; a plant that's shaded at 1 PM may be fully exposed at 3 PM. Moreover, light-colored walls and hardscape can reflect light that's half as strong as direct sun. The rule of thumb is to give succulents at least four hours of bright light daily (usually full morning or late afternoon sun), and dappled shade in the heat of the day. But certain succulents will want less and others more. Factors include the time of year, your latitude and climate, and whether the succulent naturally grows as a full-sun or understory plant. When in doubt, look up the plant's requirements. Saving the label or tag makes this easier.

Succulents that are kept dry during dormancy have a better chance of surviving a cold snap than those that are wet. Sleeping plants (and roots) are more prone to rot than when actively growing. New Zealand resident Yvonne Cave creates a "winter house" for her succulents by bending a row of flexible plastic pipes into semicircles, with the ends inserted into the ground, and stretching plastic sheeting over these pipes. The plants are kept dry and flourish, and because the sheeting extends only halfway to the ground, she's able to see and enjoy her plants all winter. Additional options for overwintering succulents include tenting them with frost cloth (available at garden centers) or growing them within cold frames or inside a greenhouse.

One way to provide succulents with a frost blanket in winter and dappled shade in summer is to plant them under trees. A good-looking tree with requirements similar to those of many succulents is Bailey's acacia (*Acacia baileyana*). I have several of variety 'Purpurea' in my garden. Their feathery blue-gray leaves tipped with lavender repeat and contrast with textures and colors found in agaves, senecios, crassulas, and kalanchoes. Bailey's acacias are fast growing (to 20 feet or more), lacy, heat and cold tolerant (to 20 degrees F), easy to come by, and relatively inexpensive.

▲ One winter a hard frost melted the leaves and trunk of this paddle plant located in an exposed area of my garden, away from the temperature-moderating influences of structures and trees. Enough of the meristem (formative plant tissue) and roots remained intact that new growth emerged the following spring. However, crassulas and aeoniums with the same exposure were irreparably damaged.

▶▶ In Tucson, saguaro and opuntia cacti thrive despite temperatures that range from below freezing to well above 100 degrees F. Until desert succulents are mature enough to handle climate extremes on their own, they grow alongside rocks or beneath "nurse plants" that provide shade in the summer and a warmer microclimate in winter.

Structures designed to provide shade can be beautiful in their own right and create mesmerizing light-and-shadow lines. As the sun moves overhead, these shift ever so slightly, and therefore are a type of kinetic art. At the Phoenix Botanical Garden, a simple canvas structure above a mammillaria collection creates an appealing scalloped shade pattern. At the Arizona-Sonora Desert Museum, my husband found me staring at bold lines on hardscape formed by slats overhead. And at Tohono Chul Park in Tucson, overlapping sheets of tough, translucent fabric ("sun sails") glow beautifully when viewed from below. When seen from a few yards away, such stretched-tight triangles are as breezy and pleasing as a sailboat at sea.

Specific information on your region's particular climate challenges and how to compensate for them is readily available from members of your nearest chapter of the Cactus and Succulent Society of America (CSSA). These enthusiasts have learned how to keep the plants in their collections alive and thriving, and are happy to share their knowledge. For example, one Colorado member who lives near Boulder at an elevation of 6,000 feet reports success growing several types of opuntia, agave, and hesperaloe, among other cold-hardy succulents, in her garden. Local nurseries, garden clubs, horticultural societies, and Master Gardeners are good sources of advice and suggestions as well.

▲ Aloes, astrophytums, and pachypodiums (Madagascar palms) thrive in the Austin, Texas, greenhouse of Jeff Pavlat.

◀ Tropical cacti grow with lush abundance in a Portland, Oregon, greenhouse.

▶ Zebra plant (*Haworthia attenuata*) and other haworthias prefer shade and therefore make great houseplants.

▲ At California Cactus Center in Pasadena, shade cloth protects succulents. Ideal light produces blurred shadows; if they're sharply defined, the sun may be too harsh.

◄ These echeverias illustrate the tendency of succulents to stretch toward light (etiolate), a phenomenon especially noticeable when the plants form bloom spikes. If your potted succulents receive sun on one side only, rotate them once a week to ensure even exposure and balanced growth.

The well-stressed succulent

A healthy succulent that has turned from green to shades of red, yellow, or orange is "beautifully stressed." In the same way deciduous trees change color in autumn, the leaves of certain succulents take on warm hues when they're given more sun, less water, and greater heat or cold than the plants prefer. Pigments responsible for this change of color, anthocyanins, are also found in berries and fruits, and are considered powerful antioxidants.

I plant noble aloes in areas of my garden where irrigation doesn't reach. They're green in winter thanks to rain and orange in summer due to drought. Certain crassulas, notably *Crassula pubescens*, turn vivid crimson under environmental stress. Like photo paper, only foliage exposed to sunlight reddens; the rest underneath stays green. The leaves of many agaves develop lovely sunset hues only when the plants are blooming; the color is part of their swan song.

▲ Van Balen's aloe in part shade (left) and full sun (right).

▶▶ Fire sticks in part shade (left) and full sun (right).

◄ Paddle plant in part shade (left) and full sun (right).

LOW-WATER, NOT NO-WATER, PLANTS

Despite being able to survive on minimal rainfall in arid climates, most succulents look best when watered regularly, especially during times of active growth. Allowing soil to go completely dry between waterings, as some advocate, may cause fine root hairs to desiccate. Consequently, a drought-stressed succulent may cease growing, lose its sheen, and not bloom. (On the plus side, such environmental stress may turn it red.) Succulents in containers will likely be fine if, during dry months, you water small pots once a week and large ones every two weeks. To flush excess salts from the soil, drench the pot until water flows out the bottom. Ideally, soil in the root zone should stay about as moist as a wrung-out sponge.

Overwatering is more of a problem for succulents than underwatering. The roots of succulents aren't designed to handle excess water. If it pools at the bottom of a container or planting hole, roots may rot—something that becomes evident when the stem has softened. If you want to try to salvage the plant, take cuttings of healthy tissue, let the cut end callus (seal itself by forming a thin membrane), and replant. Discard the old soil.

The plumper the succulent, the more water it stores and the less it needs. Cacti and rotund euphorbias are especially sensitive to overwatering—which is not surprising, considering how juicy the tissues are. Any succulent is at greater risk of rotting during dormancy; the roots of sleeping plants require little water.

It's more difficult to prevent overwatering of succulents in the garden than in pots. If your area receives more than 20 inches of rainfall a year, plant succulents atop mounded soil well amended with pumice to enhance drainage. If you live in an area of high humidity, such as the southern United States and Florida, succulents planted outdoors need to be watered less than if they were growing in a region of low humidity like the desert Southwest. A constantly moist environment is not natural for dry-climate plants; it promotes pests that thrive in dampness, plus mildew. Locating desert succulents in a screened sunroom with good air circulation and a dehumidifier is one option, as is opting for succulents that like more water than most. These include tropical cacti, many of which come from Brazilian rainforests; and those with minimal storage capacity (such as fine-leaved sedums).

Surprisingly, nondraining containers, though not ideal, are fine for succulents if you underwater them. The key is to water only enough to keep the plants healthy. Use distilled water so salts don't build up in the soil. I dribble a little water onto succulents in nondraining containers about half as often as I water succulents in pots that do have drainage. Or I let the plants tell me when they're gasping: foliage loses its luster and fine wrinkles appear at leaf tips. Don't leave nondraining containers where rain or automatic irrigation will soak them. This sounds obvious, but I know at least one person who has done it (me).

▲ I group nondraining containers to help me remember not to overwater them. Sometimes when these cacti are watered, the soil is so dry it hisses. Although I consider such plantings temporary, those shown here have been fine for over a year.

▶ Layers of sand in a trifle dish suggest both desert and dessert. Coarse sand and stones in the top create a miniature landscape that features aeoniums and treelike *Crassula tetragona*. The designer used a funnel (a cone she made of heavy paper) to place colored sand along the inside of the glass. A nondraining composition like this should be watered very minimally.

◀ Do you suppose this offset is trying to tell us something? Appropriately, its common name is walking sansevieria.

▶ Each century plant pup has the potential to become as large as the mother plant (this one is striped *Agave americana* 'Marginata'). Pups can be dug up and disposed of, a garden chore akin to weeding. Having contended with this, I now grow century plants only in pots—sturdy ones, because roots that swell as they grow can break a flimsy container.

PROPAGATING YOUR SUCCULENTS

Elephants in Africa lumber through stands of elephant's food (*Portulacaria afra*), breaking limbs that subsequently take root. Succulents—all plants, for that matter—*want* to reproduce. You don't need a laboratory, plastic gloves, or rooting hormone. If an elephant can propagate a succulent, so can you.

Although most succulents can be grown from seed, it's a lot of bother (not to mention a test of your patience: you can wait forever for a plant to become thumb sized). I don't recommend it unless there is no other way to get the succulent you want. The vast majority start readily from cuttings or offsets.

It's possible for cuttings to go directly into the garden, but you risk sun scorch or rot if you don't coddle them a bit first. This simple, intermediate step assures that a higher percentage of cuttings will become healthy rooted plants: root

them first in a black plastic nursery flat—or any shallow tray that drains—filled with potting mix. If the flat has large gaps through which soil can fall, first line the bottom with salvaged window screen or paper towels. Larger cuttings can go into soil-filled nursery pots.

To propagate shrublike succulents, use a knife, garden clippers, or kitchen scissors to cut stems 2 or 3 inches below their tips. Next, gently snap off the lowest leaves. Set cuttings in a dry, cool, shady spot for a few days until the raw tissue heals (forms a callus). Insert cuttings into the soil-filled flat. Roots will emerge from growth nodes (which resemble potato eyes) where leaves once were attached, and/or from a ring of tissue inside the skin.

With some succulents, notably aloes, lowest leaves may shrivel and dry, and hug the stem instead of falling off. When you peel away

▶ Nearly everything in my own garden (including my dog) began as a cutting, pup, or offset.

◄ A young specimen of *Agave franzosinii*, recently liberated from its container, illustrates that even potted agaves pup.

▶ Variegated aloe (*Aloe variegata*) with offspring.

the dry leaves, you may see roots or the bumps that precede them. Cut the stem below where these appear, let the raw end heal for a day or more, then bury the cutting up to the base of the rosette (the lowest pair of healthy leaves).

If the succulent is a stemless rosette, chances are it forms offsets—small plants that are attached to the parent plant in one of several ways: at the tips of underground rhizomes, along a shared stem (like Brussels sprouts), or via slender stems (like spacewalking astronauts). Offsets are ready to be pulled, wiggled, dug, or cut loose when roots descend from the base. Peel away any dry leaves and plant.

Agave pups start out as pointed tips of white rhizomes that run parallel to the soil surface. These turn upward, become green when exposed to sunlight, and grow into miniatures of the mother plant. In time, they also send out recon-

naissance rhizomes, and soon there are grand-pups. A few—notably century plant—are sneaky about it, producing pups that may surface 3 or more feet away. Pups may pop up in a neighbor's yard, in a pathway, on a slope, or on the other side of a hedge (to name a few of many possible locations).

Place a flat of cuttings or offsets in bright shade and keep soil barely moist. It's normal for succulents that lack roots to lose their sheen over time and appear the worse for wear. They'll be fine once new roots take hold and start sending water and nutrients back into the leaves. In four to six weeks—more rapidly during the growth season—they will have rooted and can be planted into the garden.

Echeveria cultivars, graptoverias, grap-topetalums, many aeoniums, some aloes, and fox tail agave (*Agave attenuata*) are among the

▲ Because this ghost plant (*Graptopetalum paraguayense*) stem is full of moisture and nutrients, roots have sprouted from leaf nodes. When a broken branch like this lands on friable (crumbly) soil, it plants itself.

▶ Plantlets along the leaf margins of bryophyllums (a type of kalanchoe) fall and root—hence the name "mother of thousands."

many succulents that grow at the tips of ever-lengthening stems. As new leaves form at the centers of the rosettes, the oldest leaves wither and dry, and may or may not fall off. These dry leaves protect the plant's stem from cold or sunburn. If those are not concerns and you prefer a tidier look, peel off the dry leaves. You can then cut the stem an inch or so below the rosette, let the cut end heal, and replant it as a cutting. Do not discard the headless plant right away; it may produce new rosettes from leaf axils.

How to have more ruffled echeverias than you know what to do with

The small backyard of Marylyn Henderson's Oceanside, CA, home was so full of potted echeverias, I had to turn sideways to squeeze past them. On tiered shelves beneath shade cloth were cabbage-sized rosettes in colors that ranged from metallic blue-gray to pale peach. Most were satin smooth, but a few were powdery or as bumpy as a bubble bath. Rising from the centers of some were foot-long flower spikes that curled toward each other, forming hearts. Each plant was a perfect specimen, and I knew many had won trophies at Cactus and Succulent Society of America shows. Horticulturists had come from as far away as Australia to see and photograph the collection.

My own ruffled echeveria, despite having broad and healthy crimson leaves, was not as glorious. The rosette perched atop a stem that resembled a vacuum cleaner hose. I showed it to Marylyn and asked her what to do about it.

"It needs beheading," she replied. She went into her house, returned with a kitchen knife, sliced cleanly through the plant's neck an inch below the lower leaves, then set the rosette atop an empty nursery pot with its bottom leaves resting on the rim. "Keep it out of the sun," Marylyn said, handing it back to me. "In a few weeks, or whenever roots form, pot it up."

She also recommended I tend the beheaded trunk as I would any potted plant. "New little rosettes may sprout from leaf axils—two or three per stem." She gestured to several potted trunks I hadn't noticed. Each had a rosette or two the size of a baby's ear.

Not long after my visit, Marylyn, a widow in her eighties, decided she wanted to live closer to one of her family members. She put her house up for sale, and because of the difficulty of transporting her collection, sold it. The income from her life's work financed the move.

I phoned to see how she was doing. Did she miss her plants? "Well," she said cheerfully, "they teach you how to propagate, but they don't teach you how to stop." During the six months it took her house to sell, she had continued to tend the stems of the rooted heads she had sold. On moving day, Marylyn snapped off the small rosettes, tossed them into a cardboard box, and discarded the potted stems. At her new home she planted the little echeverias, thereby regaining her entire collection.

▲ A caruncled echeveria in need of beheading. The weight of the rosette has caused the trunk to become pendant.

▲ Beheading an echeveria takes about two seconds.

◀ New plants grow from a beheaded stem's leaf nodes, which also are capable of producing roots.

How long cuttings remain viable depends on how much moisture they store in their tissues. A succulent cutting several inches long with leaves attached, with a stem about ½-inch in diameter, will be viable for weeks if kept in bright shade. Depending on the type of cutting, its lower leaves may dry and fall off, upper ones may stretch, and the stem may curl and become whiskered with aerial roots.

Cuttings of large, moisture-rich succulents, such as columnar euphorbias and cacti, can be set aside and planted months later. They will seal their cut ends and go dormant, neither growing nor shriveling. The original plant, once truncated, may produce new limbs around the edges of the cut end. These enlarge over time like upright water balloons attached to a garden hose.

The more egglike a succulent's leaf (such as those of aptly named *Pachyphytum oviferum*), the more likely it is to snap off and grow roots and beadlike leaves from the stem end. To help this along, place it beneath the mother plant or set the leaf atop a pot or nursery flat filled with soil. There's no need to moisten the soil or bury the leaf (lest it rot). Just as a tadpole subsists on stored nutrients—gradually growing legs and absorbing its tail—so do tiny plants feed off a leaf, which once drained resembles a raisin. When the leaf's roots find and penetrate soil, they anchor and sustain the new plant, which can then be watered.

▲ A thumb-sized sedum leaf that fell into an open bag of potting soil has sprouted roots.

▶▶ **LEFT** When an aeonium's center elongates, it's getting ready to flower. Pruning doesn't prevent this.

▶▶ **RIGHT** *Agave desmettiana* is a beautiful landscape plant, but it tends to flower at a younger age than most agaves—four to six years.

Uh-oh, your agave's blooming

Aeoniums, most agaves, and sempervivums are monocarpic, meaning they die after blooming. Once the center of the rosette begins to elongate, there's no persuading it not to flower. Cutting it off won't stop the inevitable, so you might as well enjoy the show. With aeoniums and sempervivums, not all rosettes on a plant or in a colony flower at once, so there is little loss in terms of aesthetics. Agaves are another matter. A large agave postbloom can be challenging to remove, so be sure to situate the plant wisely in the first place.

Most agaves take years to mature and flower, and bloom spikes are impressively large in proportion to the plant. As it gears up for reproduction, an agave pumps its life force into an asparagus-like stalk. Leaves at the base wither as the stalk attains what can be, with an immense agave, the height of a sailboat mast. Buds along the bloom spike—which may or may not be branched, depending on the species—become flowers. Depending on the variety of agave, these may turn into thousands of baby plants (bulbils), each a miniature of its mother. The dying agave's flower stalk eventually falls over, propelling its offspring to the ground, where some take root and continue the cycle.

Uh-oh, your agave's blooming, CONTINUED

◀ Flowers along a bloom spike of fox tail agave have become plantlets, ready to root.

▼ The bloom spike of century plant can be a foot or more in diameter. Leaves trimmed from the dying plant give the stump the look of a pineapple. Small agaves at its base are pups the plant produced earlier.

▶▶ The unbranched bloom spike of 'Blue Flame' agave arches over plant hybridizer Kelly Griffin.

DIGGING IN AND POTTING UP

Garden soil may be adequate for in-ground plants but is likely too dense for use in pots, plus it may contain weed seeds or pathogens. In a confined environment, whatever isn't ideal can become health threatening.

The bagged "cactus mix" available at any nursery or garden center is a good option if you're doing only a few pots. If you intend to do more than that or are planting an in-ground bed, it's more economical to make your own mix. This also allows greater leeway with ingredients. There are many soil formulas; it seems whomever you talk to has a slightly different one. Most include some amendment that lightens the soil and enhances drainage. I simply mix pumice (a crushed volcanic rock) with any inexpensive bagged potting soil. (Perlite can be substituted for pumice; in fact, some growers prefer it. I don't like it because it floats.) Pumice is sold at many nurseries, but I buy it by the 40-pound bag at tack-and-feed stores. One brand is Dry Stall, a product that keeps horse stalls muck free. To encourage quicker, lusher growth, I may add compost—one-third potting mix, one-third pumice, one-third compost.

A half-and-half mix of pumice or perlite and potting soil is suitable for all succulents; in fact, most will grow in pure pumice or in potting mix without pumice. However, there's a greater chance of plump succulents staying too wet when grown in pure potting soil, and of delicate-leaved succulents drying out too quickly if grown in pure pumice. Let common sense guide you, and adjust the ratio according to the plant: the fatter and fleshier the succulent, the more pumice in the mix. For example, give cacti and rotund euphorbias 70 percent pumice to 30 percent potting soil; fine-leaved sedums, 70 percent potting soil to 30 percent pumice. If you're combining plump- and thin-leaved succulents, simply go with half-and-half. Mound the soil and place plants that need more moisture around the bottom and those that need less at the top.

Slide the succulent out of its nursery pot, taking care not to break it at the crown (where stem and roots meet). Tease apart the roots. If they are so long that they don't easily fit into the new pot, or if they're coiled, clip them back. Remove any weeds that hitchhiked. Pups or offsets needn't be separated from the mother plant, but this is a convenient time to do so.

Next, place the root-ball atop potting soil in the container. You may want the plant to sit low enough in the container to allow the rim to form a dam to hold in water and topdressing. Or you may want the plant higher than the rim, perhaps supported by other plants or rocks, giving the composition a fuller, mounded look. Scoop out some soil to lower the root-ball; add more to elevate it. Cover the roots up to the crown, pressing soil firmly around it with your fingertips. The next step is to water the plant to settle the roots and wash the leaves, but because succulents store water in their leaves and stems, it's not necessary to do this right away. Ideally, give roots, especially those of cacti and euphorbias, a few days to heal first.

Get in-ground succulents off to a good start with an initial application of high-nitrogen fertilizer watered in well, followed by weekly soakings until plants are established (four or five months) unless rainfall is adequate. If you're planting on a steep slope, dig a pocket above the plant to hold water; it'll percolate downward to the root zone.

Keep dirt and leaf litter out of the centers of rosette succulents, lest the debris accumulate

▶ A side yard is the perfect location for a potting table, especially if it is near a hose bib. This table, supported by pipes (the kind used for chimneys) that double as storage bins, includes a dog-grooming area.

▼ Amending regular potting soil with pumice (shown here) is an easy and inexpensive way to make your own "cactus mix."

How to refresh an overgrown container composition

Over time, a container composition that once looked tidy and compact can become leggy and disheveled. It's easy to revitalize, due to the fact that succulents start readily from cuttings. Here I describe how I refreshed the pictured container. Note this lazy-gardener shortcut: I let the cuttings callus in dry soil, rather than following the conventional wisdom of setting them aside to heal for a few days before planting. However, the latter is the best way to go if the plants are valuable to you and you want to make sure no microbes enter raw tissue.

1. Cut off the tips (about 4 inches) of the graptosedum stems. Set cuttings aside.
2. Pull the echeveria rosette out of the bowl, root-ball and all, taking care not to mar the inner leaves. Trim away the lower, dry, unsightly ones. Set the echeveria aside.
3. Salvage any nice clumps of the sedum, roots and all. Set aside.
4. Empty the pot, discarding old soil and what remains of the original plants.
5. Fill the pot with fresh potting soil.
6. Tuck the echeveria's root-ball and stem into the soil. This composition is asymmetrical, but you could put the rosette in the center of the bowl. Rocks, which are useful for weighing down roots and propping newly planted cuttings, are optional.
7. Cluster the graptosedum cuttings around the echeveria. Pull off lower leaves on the cuttings' stems before inserting them into the soil.
8. Fill gaps with the sedum, pushing the root-balls into the soil with a chopstick.
9. For a finishing touch, cover any bare soil with pebbles or gravel.
10. Water lightly. In a week or two, once cuttings form roots, water the composition as often as you do your other potted succulents.

◀◀▼ It took about five minutes to refresh this 12-inch-diameter succulent bowl. Plants are 'California Sunset' graptosedum, 'Afterglow' echeveria, and small-leaved 'Cape Blanco' sedum. The same method would work with other rosette and trailing succulents.

and harbor insects or lead to rot. I use long-handled tweezers to remove pine needles, dead leaves, and bits of soil. Hosing larger succulents, such as in-ground agaves, is a quick and easy way to clean them.

The smoother and darker the leaf, the more obvious mineral deposits left by hard water will be. If such white spots are unpleasantly prominent, wipe them away with a soft cloth moistened with distilled water.

Avoid touching leaves that have a natural coating of white powder. There's no replacing it, and you'll leave finger marks. Without the powder, the plant will appear dull green.

In some cases, frost-damaged leaves, which turn soft and putty colored, should be removed lest they invite rot into the crown. But if frost has burned the ends of the leaves only—often the case with aloes and agaves—do not prune until spring, as tips will protect healthy tissue lower down. For aesthetic reasons, rather than cutting the tip straight across, snip it at an angle to create a point that follows the shape of the leaf.

If you need to prune the sharply pointed leaves of a large agave that is encroaching on a driveway or walkway, it's best to cut the leaf all the way to where it emerges, flush with the trunk. Cutting a leaf partway back will spoil the look of the plant.

▲ The crown of this 'Kiwi' aeonium is about half an inch below the rim of the pot.

▶▶ A graptopetalum already damaged by hail has become colonized by mealybugs. When an infestation is this extensive, it's best to discard the plant.

PART ONE: ENJOYING, GROWING, AND DESIGNING WITH SUCCULENTS

PEST AND DISEASE PATROL

Be vigilant where snails and slugs are concerned. Chewed leaves can compromise a succulent's beauty for years. There are numerous snail-control options, but the most earth friendly are handpicking, baits that contain iron phosphate (one brand is Sluggo), and predator (decollate) snails if allowed in your area; check with your local Master Gardeners organization.

Also stay on top of aphids, mealybugs, spider mites, and thrips. Aphids are pinhead-sized sucking insects that colonize tender new growth and flower buds. Mealybugs resemble bits of cotton and hide in leaf axils (where leaves join stems). Spider mites thrive in hot, dry conditions, look like cayenne pepper, and spin webs. Thrips cluster on blooms. Good air circulation generally keeps these pests at bay, but should

they set up shop, an earth-friendly control is spraying isopropyl (rubbing) alcohol diluted half-and-half with distilled water. In the case of root mealybugs, discard the infested soil, clean the container thoroughly, and take cuttings of the plant (if desired) before bagging it for the trash. Start cuttings in fresh soil.

Scale is more difficult to deal with; these bugs live inside hard brown shells. These are oval and about $\frac{1}{8}$ inch long, and they latch onto stems. Unless the plant is valuable to you, dig it out, place it in a plastic bag, tie the top, and set it out with the trash. If you can't bear to do this, wash the plant thoroughly with soapy water, gently scraping off the scale. If it's a container plant, remove it from the pot before washing. Hose off the roots and thoroughly clean the

◀ A type of mite that affects aloes makes tissues distorted and bubbly looking, with an orange tinge.

Seasonal care for succulents

An in-ground garden in USDA plant hardiness zones 8 to 11 (based on the average annual minimum winter temperature; see "Metric Conversions and Plant Hardiness Zones" for more information) comprised primarily of succulents needs maintaining on average four times a year. The plants may need to be thinned, deadheaded, and have old leaves or branches removed; any that aren't thriving, replaced; weeds and pests dealt with; and trimmings not suitable for planting, hauled away. If you're unable to do this yourself, check with landscape professionals who design and install succulent gardens to see if they offer seasonal maintenance.

FALL

As the weather cools and the days shorten, succulents start to nod off. Most will require little attention for months, other than protection from frost and excess rain. However, certain winter growers are waking up—mainly senecios, aeoniums, and sempervivums. If these are overgrown and leggy, trim them back and start cuttings. Fall is also the time to start lesser-known winter-growing succulents such as tylecodons, othonnas and certain aloes, notably *Aloe plicatilis* and *Aloe dichotoma*.

WINTER

As your succulents go dormant, keep them on the dry side and don't fertilize. If you live in zone 8 or lower, decide how to shelter the plants from excessive rain and freezing temperatures. Sempervivums and sedums (with the exception of larger-leaved sedums from Mexico) are fine outdoors in zone 5 and above. Semps prefer dry cold, so rather than leaving their containers where rain will soak them, move them beneath an eave.

pot. Repot in fresh soil and quarantine the plant for several months. Also check other succulents in your collection, especially those close by, for signs of infestation.

Aloes are susceptible to a microscopic mite that causes orangey, cancerous-looking growth near the stem. Cut out the infected tissue and isolate the aloe until new growth proves that the infestation is gone. Clean your tools so you don't spread the mite to other aloes.

Another aloe disease (which also affects gasterias) pockmarks the leaves, creating unsightly black depressions surrounded by bruised-looking tissue. Mix 2 tablespoons ground cinnamon per pint of isopropyl alcohol, shake well, let infuse overnight, strain through a coffee filter, and spray the plants with the brown liquid. If this doesn't solve the problem, your only recourse may be to apply one of the many systemic disease controls sold at nurseries and garden centers.

Agave snout-nosed weevil causes agaves to wilt, leaving the central core upright. The affected plant should be disposed of and a systemic insecticide applied to any agaves, mangaves, and yuccas nearby, and to the surrounding soil as well (if it's too difficult to remove and dispose of it). Unfortunately, there is no organic control.

SPRING

As the weather warms and succulents you've overwintered indoors emerge from dormancy, gradually increase water and sunlight as they become acclimated to the outdoors. For best form, growth, and color, most succulents need a minimum of four hours of sun daily (except the few shade lovers). To stimulate growth of container plants, apply a liquid fertilizer diluted half-and-half with water. Fertilize garden succulents if you like, but some experts say it isn't necessary. Cuttings taken now from spring or summer growers—the majority of succulents—will root quickly.

SUMMER

If you live in the Southwest, move your container-grown succulents into greater shade, reducing the number of hours they spend in hot sun. Keep in mind that the smaller the pot, the more quickly the soil is likely to dry out, especially if the container is a porous material like terracotta. Don't be concerned if sempervivums, echeverias, dudleyas, and aeoniums close their rosettes to protect themselves from sun and heat damage. Beige patches on leaves indicate sunburn; this is seldom fatal, but sunburned leaves don't recover and can be unsightly. If you water thoroughly before leaving on vacation, your succulents should be fine for up to two weeks, providing they're well established, are out of broiling sun, and temperatures stay below 90 degrees F. Echeverias, kalanchoes, and small aloes are better over- than underwatered in summer (providing drainage is superb), so if possible, place them where they'll receive automatic irrigation while you're away.

What's wrong with your succulent?

Here are some troubleshooting tips for common afflictions and conditions.

SYMPTOM Bleached, beige, or dark patches on leaves
CAUSE Excessive sun exposure
REMEDY Move plants into bright shade. Remove damaged leaves if unsightly.

SYMPTOM Distorted buds that don't open, tiny insects on new growth
CAUSE Aphids or thrips
REMEDY Spray with isopropyl alcohol diluted half-and-half with water and improve air circulation.

SYMPTOM Cancerous growth on aloes
CAUSE Aloe mite
REMEDY Cut out the damaged tissue, clean your tools, and if the plant is potted, isolate it from other aloes.

SYMPTOM Distorted growth at leaf axils and centers of rosettes, cottony bits
CAUSE Mealybug
REMEDY Remove or isolate affected plants; spray with diluted isopropyl alcohol and improve air circulation.

SYMPTOM Cottony bits adhering to roots
CAUSE Root mealybug
REMEDY Discard the affected soil; wash the container in soapy water; take cuttings of the plant and repot in fresh soil.

SYMPTOM Black depressions in aloe leaves
CAUSE Bacterial leaf spot
REMEDY Apply cinnamon spray or commercial systemic per label directions.

SYMPTOM Webs and paprika-like dots on leaves
CAUSE Red spider mite
REMEDY Spray with diluted isopropyl alcohol and improve air circulation.

SYMPTOM Sickly look, brown bumps on stems
CAUSE Scale insects
REMEDY Remove or isolate affected plants, spray with diluted isopropyl alcohol, scrape the scale off stems with a plastic knife, wash the plant with mild liquid detergent, and repot it in fresh soil.

SYMPTOM Collapsed outer leaves, upright center (agaves)
CAUSE Agave snout weevil
REMEDY Dig up and destroy the affected plant. Do not replant agaves in or near that area. Treat nearby agaves and soil with systemic insecticide.

SYMPTOM Holes in leaves
CAUSE Snails and slugs
REMEDY Hand pick; release predator snails or apply iron phosphate (Sluggo).

SYMPTOM Garden plants cropped to ground level
CAUSE Deer, squirrels, rabbits, or javelinas
REMEDY Enclose young, tender plants in chicken-wire cages.

SYMPTOM Collapsed, putty-colored leaves
CAUSE Frost
REMEDY Tent in-ground plants with frost cloth until the temperature exceeds 32 degrees F. Move containers beneath shelter or indoors. Prune dead tissue.

SYMPTOM Squishy stem or trunk
CAUSE Overwatering
REMEDY Take cuttings from healthy tissue and replant. Discard the old soil with the plant.

SYMPTOM Loss of sheen, shriveling at tips
CAUSE Underwatering
REMEDY Water thoroughly and then keep soil about as moist as a wrung-out sponge.

SYMPTOM Elongated, stretched-looking stems and leaves; flattened or downward-curving rosettes
CAUSE Not enough light
REMEDY Give greater sun incrementally. Rotate container weekly for even exposure.

SYMPTOM Greening of yellow, red, or orange leaves
CAUSE Too much pampering
REMEDY Stress the plant with less water, more sun, and less rich soil. Don't fertilize.

SYMPTOM Irregular white rings on dark leaves
CAUSE Mineral deposits from evaporated water drops
REMEDY Using distilled water, gently wipe the leaves. Avoid splashing the leaves when watering the plant.

SYMPTOM Dry leaves at base of echeverias, aloes, or other rosette succulents
CAUSE Normal growth
REMEDY Crisp, papery leaves shade and insulate the stem. But if you find them unsightly, peel them away.

SYMPTOM Stem awkwardly long with rosette at the tip
CAUSE Normal growth
REMEDY Remove any old, dry leaves at the base of the rosette, then cut the stem 1 inch below healthy leaves and replant the rosette as a cutting.

SYMPTOM Closed or shrunken rosettes
CAUSE Heat, drought, or cold; dormancy
REMEDY Move container-grown plants under an eve or overhang to protect from harsh outdoor conditions. If plants are merely dormant, leave them alone; they'll revive when they awaken.

Composing Great-Looking Succulent Gardens and Containers

WHETHER YOU'RE LANDSCAPING a garden, doing a potted arrangement, or creating a succulent bouquet, aim to use succulents in aesthetic ways that delight you and those with whom you share them. As you work—and play—toward that goal, you'll define and enhance your individual style.

This chapter demystifies good design so you'll recognize it when you see it and hopefully be inspired to emulate it. Of course, it's highly subjective. My criterion often is: Would I see it in *Sunset* or *Better Homes & Gardens*? Compositions that publications show their readers invariably have in common certain design fundamentals. These can be learned. Raw talent is helpful, but anyone who has a keen interest can become competent, have fun, and experience creative fulfillment.

The best design, while firmly based in fundamentals, innovates. It's in keeping with the designer's style yet different from what's been done before and may even be a bit quirky. Whenever I visit a garden or nursery, I never know what I'll find; my motto is, "If it's beautiful, shoot it." My antennae quiver when I detect a trend, a clever method, or a subtle embellishment that makes a big difference.

Certain things are turnoffs. Some are obvious, such as weeds or plants with chewed leaves and dead blooms. Others, less so. For example, it may come as a surprise that publication-worthy gardens seldom incorporate anything plastic. (If you do nothing but get rid of plastic items in your garden, you'll make a giant stride forward.) Bare dirt is also anathema—and unnecessary when gravel, decomposed granite, or other topdressings are available. Yet even when it comes to bare dirt and plastic, no doubt there are exceptions.

I collect one-of-a-kind, artist-designed pots, but I also enjoy scouring secondhand stores for items that can be repurposed as containers for succulents. Figuring out how to modify them is much of the fun. However, my guiding principle is that all pots should showcase the plants. Containers are merely backup singers.

Succulents may be the most obliging of plants, but as living entities, they occasionally have minds of their own. Any garden, whether in teacup or trough, is never static; plants are continually changing. It's intriguing to see what they're capable of, and satisfying to watch them grow and thrive. Fine-tuning your designs is part of this, as is learning as you go along.

◀◀ Consider the size, shape and color of your pot when selecting succulents to plant in it. Here, a large caruncled echeveria is in scale with a tall pot. The filler plant, red 'Campfire' crassula, provides contrasting color and form. Spilling over the sides is 'Fish Hooks' senecio, which repeats the blue in the echeveria.

DESIGN BASICS: SCALE, REPETITION, AND CONTRAST

The best way to gain confidence in your design abilities is to start with container compositions. As you create a few and observe those you see in photos and at homes and nurseries, you'll realize how basic design principles can apply to any garden, large or small.

First consider scale and proportion. This means choosing a container that relates effectively to the location in which it will go and selecting succulents sized correctly for the pot—one reason Part Three's top 100 list includes each plant's size at maturity. One large container is often more visually pleasing than a lot of small ones, but don't be overly concerned about that now. Large pots are an investment,

and grouping smaller ones can create a similar effect.

The easiest way to improve the look of anything you do—from selecting a scarf or necktie to pairing pots and plants—is to keep in mind repetition and contrast. Once you "get" those concepts, everything else will fall into place. You'll use color deliberately and no longer feel overwhelmed by choices.

It's aesthetically pleasing to see the same plant or design element repeated—such as barrel cacti amid boulders, crimson pots with red aloes, or silver echeverias with silver 'Powis Castle' artemesia. Repetition is soothing. It works up to a point and then becomes tedious;

▶ An urn atop a pedestal at the San Francisco Decorator Showcase is in scale with the mansion and in keeping with its classical revival architecture. The composition, which includes aeoniums, echeverias, and lampranthus, has as its focal point an aloe that curls downward, emphasizing the line of the bowl. The arrangement also repeats the size and shape of the urn (in reverse).

◀◀ Bring your pots with you when you shop for plants. I go down the aisles carrying a container, the better to see what goes with it.

this is when contrast, which is exciting, comes into play. For example, in a multiple planting of agaves and yuccas, the addition of airy ornamental grasses is refreshing. Or you might add a plant that contrasts with the agaves' fountain shape and blue-gray color, such as orange-red 'Sticks on Fire' euphorbia.

Since the leaves of succulents come in nearly every color, it's likely possible to repeat a hue found in the pot you've chosen. Color-wheel complements are also effective. (On a color wheel, a *complement* is the opposite color.) Contrast blue with orange, yellow with purple, and red with green. It's also appealing to repeat and juxtapose primary colors (red, yellow, and blue); secondary colors (orange, purple, and green); and pastels.

Succulents offer opportunities for repetition and contrast of shapes and textures, as well. The plants' bold forms include cylinders, balls, stars, fountains, fans, paddles, and more. Textures range from smooth and glossy to whiskery and spiky.

Because their leaf shapes are distinctly pointed, oval, or cylindrical, succulents—perhaps more than all other plants—offer opportunities for crisply defined repetitions of form. Designers refer to these harmonious, recurring patterns as a garden's *rhythms*. They have the same soothing effect as a musical motif; in fact, when I see such repetitions in a well-designed garden, I hear music.

Repetition can be a difficult principle for plant collectors who want one of everything and

◀ One way to add a high-design look to your succulent garden is to include golden barrel cactus (*Echinocactus grusonii*). The butter-yellow balls offer wonderful texture and a dynamic, spherical shape.

▼ The cactus in this perfect plant-pot pairing is one of the most common, *Mammillaria elongata*, known as lady fingers because the spines are harmless—it's one of the "pettable" cacti.

▼ **SUCCULENT COLOR WHEEL** In addition to all shades of green, succulent leaves come in nearly every color (deep blue is the exception), including intense hues and soft pastels. Leaves also can be silver, gray, white, and a burgundy so dark it looks black.

SUNSET JADE

FIRE STICKS EUPHORBIA

SEMPERVIVUM

ALOE

AGAVE

ECHEVERIA

◀ It's visually exciting when plants in a vignette have several elements in common yet also embody dramatic differences. Here, the bristles of spiny euphorbia (*Euphorbia atrispina*) emphasize the 'Voodoo' aenonium's glossy leaves. Colors are green and maroon; forms, rounded and upright. In spring, the euphorbia's yellow, beadlike blooms add another element of contrast—and repetition, because aeoniums produce yellow flowers as well.

▲ The crisp lines of *Agave desmettiana* 'Variegata' contrast with softly rounded 'Sunburst' aeonium rosettes. Yellow-and-green repeats.

▶▶ Large furcraeas, which are in the agave family, create drama in a serpentine garden bed. One furcraea would be lovely, but repeating several is amazing. Note, too, that the soil in the beds is mounded, which is more interesting than flat. Tall plants serve as a backdrop to smaller ones. Aloes (in bloom) give definition to a river of foliage and repeat the furcraeas' multipointed silhouette.

see no point in having extras. But repetition is essential for unifying a garden. Large agaves, in particular, illustrate this: Just three of them, all the same and strategically placed, will lend continuity to a landscape regardless of its other components. And if those agaves are variegated, so much the better; their striped leaves will provide another motif.

Repetition is not always multiples of the same plant. It can be achieved in subtler ways, via patterns and silhouettes. A yucca planted near an agave shares the same spiky shape, as do tufts of blue fescue at its base. Color, too, is an effective way of playing the same tune with multiple instruments. Combine *Senecio serpens*, *Agave parryi*, *Crassula arborescens*, and *Festuca glauca*, and you have four-part harmony sung in silvery blue.

Anything aligned, straight, or right angled announces human intervention; in nature, plants seldom grow in rows or grids. Gardens with plants equidistant from each other and parallel to, say, the curb tend to indicate a homeowner oblivious to this tendency. When you find yourself doing it, make a conscious effort not to, and see if you like the results better. Then, as an exercise in design, plant a geometric arrangement of mammillaria, astrophytums, or barrel cacti. When done with intent, such repetitions can be Zenlike in their simplicity and perfectly showcase the plants' forms. You might compose a geometric garden in a level area of your yard, or a linear one in identical pots—especially if your home's architecture is contemporary.

◀ Blues repeat in the fingerlike ground cover, the striped century plant (*Agave americana* 'Marginata'), and knobby blue-gray *Cereus peruvianus* 'Monstrosus'. Shapes and textures contrast, as does the color yellow.

▶ Red-orange 'Campfire' crassula contrasts with propeller plant (*Crassula perfoliata* var. *falcata*) in a garden bed. Red also unifies the composition; it's found in the crown of thorns (*Euphorbia milii*), paddle plant, and 'Calico Kitten' crassula (lower left).

▼ Golden ball cactus (*Parodia leninghausii*) is intriguing when planted in a grid. Would you choose a square pot for this, or circular? A case could be made for either.

▲ A blue pot containing red-orange *Aloe cameronii* is framed by similarly hot-hued 'California Sunset' graptosedum.

▶ Tawny coppertone stonecrop contrasts with blue *Pilosocereus pachycladus*, and with our Lord's candle (*Yucca whipplei*), which in turn repeats the color of the wall. Textures contrast as well: the cactus is fuzzy, the yucca pointed, and the sedum smooth.

Checklist for a gorgeous succulent garden

- Evaluate plants, pots, and enhancements such as boulders in terms of how their size and shape fit their prospective location. Are they so small they're lost in it or so big they overwhelm it?
- Take the containers you'll be planting to the nursery when you go. Try different succulents in them, like trying on clothes.
- Consider how you might effectively repeat or contrast colors, textures, and patterns, not only within a composition but also with non-negotiable aspects of the site.
- If you don't want to call attention to, say, a blue tarp in a neighbor's yard, don't put a pot that same blue in your yard. Repeating some aspect of an eyesore makes it more noticeable.
- Instead of creating a pancake-flat garden, bring in soil and sculpt mounds and swales.
- Consider adding a dry streambed that channels runoff or gray water into the garden.
- Instead of a straight pathway, do an S-curve.
- Avoid dotting plants or boulders equidistant from each other or aligning them, unless your intent is to make a geometric or formal arrangement.
- Mass the plants. A solo aeonium or echeveria rosette, though lovely, won't be as appealing as a cluster.
- Fill gaps between plants with decomposed granite, earth-colored gravel, or a ground cover such as ice plant, *Sedum rubrotinctum* 'Pork-and-Beans', or blue senecio.
- Add interest with rocks and boulders of various sizes and shapes.
- Combine short, medium-height, and tall plants in vignettes. Use one or more large succulents for drama and height, midsize shrubs for lushness, and low growers as ground covers.
- Create the illusion of distance by placing taller, larger items in back and smaller items in front.
- Hide some plants from view for mystery. Entice visitors to wonder what's behind a curve, hill, or berm, or down in a canyon.
- Position succulents covered in spines or filaments, or that have translucent leaf margins, where they will be backlit by early morning or late afternoon sun. Silver torch cactus will glow snowy white, aeoniums will become bright pinwheels, and 'Sticks on Fire' euphorbia will live up to its name.
- Know before you plant something how large it will grow. Agaves vary in size from soccer balls to Volkswagens. The wrong one planted too close to a driveway, gate, or sidewalk can be a menace that's difficult to remove.
- Juxtapose succulents of contrasting shapes, colors, and textures. Experiment and rearrange. Most are shallow-rooted and transplant easily, especially when small.
- When designing a patio or balcony garden, select containers that have in common material, color, texture, pattern, shape, style, or size.

▶ Newly planted beds have berms and swales, succulents of varying heights, and small and large boulders. Because water percolates downward, succulents that need less are higher than those needing more.

▼ A year and a half later, the same beds have filled in. Color, height, and textures are much more pronounced.

GETTING CREATIVE WITH COLOR

All my outdoor furniture is what I call agave green. I took a leaf to the paint store, asked them to match it, then evaluated the results in the parking lot (where it was sunny) until I was satisfied. I'm pleased with that soothing gray-green; it works with every succulent—with every plant, for that matter—in the garden.

If bright colors are more to your liking, paint a chair blue to contrast with orange-blooming aloes, or paint it crimson and situate it near a colony of red-leaved *Aloe cameronii*. If your metal outdoor furniture has a verdigris (greenish) finish, consider planting nearby succulents in celadon green glazed pots.

Your garden's most important backdrop is your house, so keep its color and architecture in mind. If it is Spanish style with a clay-tile roof, repeat that with terracotta pots, perhaps accented with handpainted Talavera pottery from Mexico. Because this pottery's designs are strong, pair it with bold succulents. If the pots have cross-hatching, echo it with the diamond-shaped leaves of stacked crassulas and sempervivums.

Nothing in a garden stands out as much as white; it shouts at the viewer like a carnival barker. Red is next. Black, on the other hand, is invisible; it reads as a shadow. White-variegated succulents are useful for brightening shady spots, and red and orange for adding pizzazz to beds viewed from a distance. If a part of your garden seems too hot and bright, cool it with blues and greens. If there's an eyesore beyond your yard, situate a white or silver focal point in the line of sight.

The more vivid the contrast, the more memorable the composition. Juxtapose blue with orange, bright red with lime green, and yellow with purple. Combine 'Zwartkop' aeonium hybrids, which have burgundy leaves and green centers, with green pots. Complementary colors need not be of the same intensity; try pairing a peach-colored plant with deep purple, or gold with lavender.

At dusk or by moonlight, a garden of silvery foliage appears to glow. Moonbeam-hued succulents include *Senecio haworthii*, *Cotyledon orbiculata*, and *Crassula arborescens*. You might add *Artemisia* 'Powis Castle'—a perennial with feathery leaves—for texture contrast.

If a pot is cobalt—one of the few colors not found in succulents—go with orange, yellow, lime green, or a plant that combines two or all three. Possible choices are *Agave lophantha* 'Quadricolor', *Aloe nobilis*, *Aloe dorotheae*, *Echeveria agavoides* 'Lipstick', *Euphorbia tirucalli* 'Sticks on Fire', *Sedum nussbaumerianum*, and *Sedum* 'Angelina'.

When in doubt, go with terracotta. It's a neutral that seems to blend with anything, including attention-grabbing colors and patterns.

▶ A red pot echoes the edges of 'Kiwi' aeonium leaves and contrasts with chartreuse 'Angelina' sedum, paddle plant, and cobweb houseleeks.

◀◀ A yellow pot pulls the color in the centers of the stacked crassula; the leaves' red margins contrast.

▲ **LEFT** Teal blue in the leaves of paddle plant is repeated in the color of the pot, which in turn is the same shape as the leaves. Red and blue contrast.

▲ **RIGHT** Terracotta, commonly used for pots, comes in shades of orange that range from peach through rust. Here, blue echeverias and upright fan aloe contrast with pale terracotta. Red peperomia adds punch.

▶ Despite the Talavera pot's boldness, *Aeonium nobile* (a choice inspired by the pattern) has no trouble getting noticed.

▲ A jardinière inspired the choice of cream-and-green 'Sunburst' aeonium and red 'Campfire' crassula.

◀ A green pot repeats the green of aeonium rosette centers and contrasts with the plant's burgundy tips.

▶ To unify a grouping of disparate pots, cross the colors: match the color of one container with a plant in another. Here, the yellow of the pot in the back repeats the yellow of jade (*Crassula ovata* 'Hummel's Sunset') in the green pot, string of pearls in the red pot harmonizes with green plants in other pots, and red stacked crassulas in the green and orange pots go with the red pot.

▼ Stems and orangey spines of *Euphorbia aeruginosa* repeat the lines and colors of its pot; green contrasts.

Ten steps to a lush and lovely container garden

1. Let the pot speak to you. What are its color, pattern, and texture? Pick an aspect that can easily be repeated in your plant selection. For example, a succulent with a wavy, channeled silhouette (such as snowflake euphorbia) might repeat a pot's rippled texture or fluted rim.

2. Look for foliage colors that are the same intensity (pastel or bright) as that of the pot. Set aside enough of your first-choice succulent to fill one-quarter to one-third of the container.

3. Check the green in the plant you chose. Is it yellow-green or blue-green? Stick with that shade of green for the rest of the composition.

4. Look for contrast in your next plant choice. This might be a color that's the complement of the first, or of the pot's glaze; a nubby-textured succulent for a glossy pot; or an angular plant in a round container. If the succulent also has an element that repeats something in the pot or the earlier plants you chose, so much the better.

5. Select tall, medium-height, and low plants, keeping contrast and repetition in mind.

6. Fill the container to 3 or 4 inches below the rim (or, if the pot is small, fill it three-quarters full). Remove the largest or tallest of the succulents from its nursery pot and place it atop the soil just off center. Press down on the root-ball to secure it but don't bury it. It's OK if the top of the root-ball is higher than the rim.

7. As you add plants, work from the middle outward, leaving cascaders for last. Push root-balls up against each other, taking care not to bruise the leaves. When you risk damaging a plant, use the blunt end of a chopstick to arrange and settle its roots.

8. Rotate rosettes that are near the rim so they face outward at a 45-degree angle. If need be, rest their crowns on the rim of the pot.

9. Conceal exposed root-balls with smaller succulents. It's fine to set one root-ball atop another. Aim for a mounded composition with no gaps. Small stones or pebbles can hide bare soil until the plants fill in.

10. Remove soil from leaves by blowing on it, dusting with a soft artist's brush, or watering gently. This last will also help settle the roots. If you must move the newly planted arrangement, do so gingerly lest a plant sitting atop another be jarred loose.

WHY YOU REALLY NEED ROCKS

Boulders serve effectively as garden focal points, provide a backdrop for sculptural succulents, offer contrasting texture, radiate warmth, and hold moisture in the soil. As a topdressing (mulch), crushed rock (gravel) conceals bare dirt, keeps weeds from germinating, and helps prevent soil erosion. The muted colors of many kinds of rocks also harmonize with succulent foliage. However, stones that have been smoothed and rounded by water may be subliminally unsettling in a succulent garden. (They beg the question: Why are they there?) Use such stones to line dry streambeds, which can double as pathways into the garden. Be wary of crushed rock that calls attention to itself, especially white or unnatural colors. When in doubt, go with gravel that's similar to rocks in the surrounding terrain.

In much the same way, finer topdressings add an important finishing touch to container gardens, unifying a composition by repeating or contrasting hues and textures found in the pot or plants. I keep 50-pound bags of pea gravel and pebbles in my potting area. They're from a masonry supplier that offers various sizes and kinds of rocks for landscapes. Other options are polished and semiprecious stones, volcanic scoria, crushed brick, recycled glass, and sifted desert sand. Look for abandoned anthills; the insects will have sifted the sand for you into piles of same-sized grains.

To help keep potting soil from coming up through a small-grained topdressing when the container is watered, add a layer of fine sand between soil and topdressing. Also, if you're using crushed glass or flattened marbles, white sand atop dark soil will keep the color of the glass true.

▼ A colorful assortment of topdressings includes tumbled glass and polished stones.

◀ A topdressing of crushed brick repeats the prickles along the edges of the leaves of a mosaic aloe (*Aloe hemmingii*). The rim of the pot adds contrast and echoes the plant's cream-colored variegation.

▼ Boulders are important compositional elements in this northern California front yard and also create a warm microclimate for the plants in winter. Included are *Aloe plicatilis* (upper right), *Agave filifera* below it, and in bloom, *Echeveria pulvinata*.

◀◀ In a mounded container composition, succulents nestle amid amethyst crystals and geodes.

▶ A mosaic of plants includes echeverias and 'Green Ice' gasteraloes surrounded by flagstone pieces inserted into the soil so only their narrow sides show. These add texture and color, and create a durable outline for the design. Topdressings are pebbles of various colors and beach glass.

PLANTS THAT PLAY WELL WITH SUCCULENTS

You need not be constrained by a solely succulent palette; there are wonderful companion plants with similar cultivation requirements. Combining drought-tolerant ornamental plants with succulents significantly increases your design options. Dozens of ornamental landscape plants perform beautifully in the same conditions in which succulents do best. These companion plants share several cultivation requirements with succulents:

- prefer soil that drains well and is moderately fertile but not necessarily richly amended
- are drought-tolerant and need minimal water once established
- do best in full sun or dappled shade (bright shade in desert areas)
- do not want a lot of rainfall or humidity
- can tolerate some frost but do best when temperatures stay above freezing
- thrive in areas with warm, dry summers

There's a chapter dedicated to companion plants in my book *Designing with Succulents*. It includes nearly a hundred, but to give you a quick reference, I've included my top thirty-five here. For greater detail on the growth habits and requirements of dry-climate plants, consult the experts at your local nursery or a trusted garden guide. As you plan your landscape, pay particular attention to how large these plants will become, and position them so they will not engulf slower-growing succulents and other plants nearby.

▲ Although succulents are beautiful backlit by the sun, with spines or prickles aglow, nothing can compare to champagnelike sprays of ornamental grasses, especially when moving in the wind. Agaves and columnar cacti contrast with airy Peruvian feather grass (*Jarava ichu*), a South American relative of Mexican feather grass (*Nassella tenuissima*). Although it is not as prone to disperse seeds as the latter, it's best to plant *Jarava ichu* only in arid locations.

▼ Statice (*Limonium perezii*), which is native to the Canary Islands (where many succulents come from, too), forms airy shrubs about 2 feet high. The strawflower-like clusters rustle pleasantly when touched and are useful in dry bouquets.

Top 35 companion plants for succulents

ANNUAL
Eschscholzia californica (California poppy)

GROUND COVER
Dymondia margaretae (dymondia)

HERBACEOUS PERENNIALS
Anigozanthos hybrids (kangaroo paw)
Artemisia 'Powis Castle' ('Powis Castle' wormwood)
Bromeliaceae species (bromeliads)
Erigeron karvinskianus (Santa Barbara daisy)
Euphorbia rigida (gopher spurge)
Gazania species (African daisies)
Hemerocallis species (daylilies)
Lavandula species (lavender)
Limonium perezii (statice)
Phormium species (New Zealand flax)
Rosa banksiae (Lady Banks rose)
Tradescantia pallida 'Purpurea' (purple heart)

ORNAMENTAL GRASSES
Festuca glauca (blue fescue)
Jarava ichu (Peruvian feather grass)

TREES AND SHRUBS
Acacia baileyana (Bailey's acacia)
Brahea armata (Mexican blue fan palm)
Butia capitata (Pindo palm)
Calliandra californica (Baja fairy duster)
Cistus species (rockrose)
Echium candicans (pride of Madeira)
Euphorbia cotinifolia (Caribbean copper plant)
Euryops pectinatus (gray-leaved euryops)
Ficus carica (edible fig)
Fouquieria macdougalii (Mexican ocotillo)
Grevillea species (grevillea)
Lantana species (lantana)
Lavatera maritima (tree mallow)
Olea europaea (olive)
Parkinsonia (*Cercidium*) 'Desert Museum' (palo verde)
Perovskia species (Russian sage)
Punica granatum (pomegranate)
Salvia species (sage)
Senna artemisioides (*Cassia artemisioides*) (feathery cassia)

◀ Airy Mexican ocotillo (*Fouquieria macdougalii*, upper right) makes a wonderful companion plant for a succulent garden, lending texture, height, and a sense of motion. When in bloom it is tipped with bright red flowers.

◀ Gazanias and ice plant bloom at the same time, in early spring.

▼ Kangaroo paws (*Anigozanthos* hybrids) with airy, fuzzy flowers in sunrise hues of orange, yellow, and red look great when juxtaposed with variegated Spanish bayonet (*Yucca aloifolia*). Kangaroo paw hybrids in the Bush Gems series have been bred to resist the root and leaf diseases that plagued their predecessors. Foliage clumps range in size from dwarfs ideal for containers to garden plants that grow up to 3 feet wide. Flower stalks that rise from strappy foliage are several feet tall.

▶ In this mild coastal garden, red bromeliads make striking companions for a variegated furcraea (left), a carpet of green 'Dondo' echeveria, and, in the pot, variegated octopus agave, purple graptopetalums, 'Afterglow' echeveria, and burro tail sedum.

EXPRESS YOUR STYLE WITH WHIMSY

As you gain confidence in your design ability, consider expressing your own brand of whimsy. Because it's as different as every individual, whimsy is hard to define. It might be as simple as a hen pot with a stacked crassula that suggests tail feathers, or as complicated as yuccas planted so their trunks become S-shaped enhancements to a dry streambed.

You'll know you've attained this elusive quality if a vignette evokes delighted gasps from guests. However, anything trite, too cute, or kitschy may have the opposite effect. Keep in mind that the best garden whimsy is subtle. It's not a whirling or bobbing object from a garden center but rather an expression of your distinctive style, sense of humor, and panache.

Because many succulents suggest undersea flora and fauna or have geometric shapes and patterns similar to seashells, combining them can create delightful beach-themed dish

Not your grandma's topiary

Topiary is a great medium for whimsy, and succulents lend themselves to it beautifully. The plants can be glued (as rosettes) onto, or inserted (as cuttings) into, forms stuffed with moss and/or soil. During the several weeks it takes for the succulents to grow roots, they draw on moisture stored in their leaves. For step-by-step projects that illustrate topiary techniques and how to glue succulents, see Part Two.

▶ A whimsical topiary "cushion" for a metal garden chair consists of moss-stuffed hardware mesh planted with several kinds of tiny sedum rosettes. Enhancing the design are a fringe of string of pearls and 'Kiwi' aeonium rosettes that suggest a floral pattern.

▶▶ Designer Laura Eubanks found a topiary alligator frame at a garage sale and glued moss and rosette succulents onto it. Spritzed with water occasionally, such topiaries are surprisingly long lasting.

gardens. Many small euphorbias in particular resemble ocean flora and fauna. Dwarf aloes, especially those that turn bright red when stressed, are sea star look-alikes. Certain agaves are squidlike. Crested cacti suggest coral. You might embellish your seabed scene with glass fish, shells, tumbled glass, lava rocks, or white sand.

▲ This life-size topiary form is packed with moss and wrapped with wire. It has an ice-plant headdress, puff sleeves of the tropical cactus *Hatiora salicornioides*, a necklace of string of pearls (*Senecio rowleyanus*), and a bustier of sempervivums, anacampseros, and English stonecrop (*Sedum anglicum*).

◀ Spanish bayonet trees (*Yucca aloifolia*) appear to sway above a dry streambed. Old leaves trimmed close to the trunks create a textural, shingled effect.

▼ For a vertical display that makes people look twice, set ¾-inch-diameter (#6) rebar in concrete in the ground to create a slender post, then thread it through the drain holes of several flower pots. Stack the pots facing different directions and fill with potting soil and succulents.

▲ An antique cast-iron dollhouse bathtub is home to cobweb houseleeks which, in this context, suggest soap bubbles.

◀ If you've been thinking of removing your lawn but don't know what to put there instead, why not a whimsical focal point? An overturned, partially buried pot appears to spill its contents: an aloe in bloom and aeoniums. Pots in the background of the same blue lend continuity.

◀ I tell my audiences they may not realize how much they like cactus. Then I show this photo, which invariably evokes smiles and pleased exclamations. The plant-pot combo perfectly exemplifies contrast, repetition, and sophisticated whimsy.

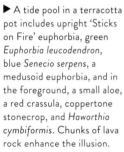

▶ A tide pool in a terracotta pot includes upright 'Sticks on Fire' euphorbia, green *Euphorbia leucodendron*, blue *Senecio serpens*, a medusoid euphorbia, and in the foreground, a small aloe, a red crassula, coppertone stonecrop, and *Haworthia cymbiformis*. Chunks of lava rock enhance the illusion.

▼ A wreath of scallop shells hot-glued to a donut-shaped wood back is ornamented with additional seashells and succulents. The root-balls are in moss-wrapped pockets of soil that can be detached from the wreath when the plants outgrow the arrangement. These pockets, which designers Cate Schotl and Kristi Collyer call "burritos," are lashed in place with fishing line.

FLEA-MARKET FINDS AND REPURPOSED CONTAINERS

Secondhand shops, flea markets, and garage sales can be sources of containers to repurpose as unconventional homes for succulents. From dainty vases and teacups to beveled gears and hubcaps, just about anything that will hold some soil or tightly packed moss and one or more plants or cuttings will work. I've seen designers use succulents in muffin tins, loaf pans, fishbowls, brandy snifters, fishing tackle boxes, red wagons, and watering cans. It depends on what appeals to you and what you run across.

Although it can be surprising what succulents will put up with, it's best to view compositions that offer less-than-ideal conditions as temporary. You needn't drill holes in the secondhand treasures you find, but it's a good idea if you intend to sell or give away your arrangements, unless your recipients understand that succulents in nondraining containers should be watered very minimally.

If the repurposed item you're planting has one or more gaps or an open bottom, cover them with a piece of window screen so soil doesn't fall out. Plastic window screen is sold by the roll at home improvement stores and may be found at suppliers of used building materials. Weed barrier cloth will also work as a liner. Succulents will last a long time without soil. This means you can place cuttings in a sugar bowl, and they'll look good for weeks. When they've begun to etiolate (stretch toward light) or lose their sheen and start to shrivel, pot up the cuttings or plant them in the garden.

If you don't want the inside of a drawer or other unconventional container to become wet or dirty, line it with plastic (use a heavy-duty trash bag). Cut the plastic slightly larger than the container, and when you're done planting, trim and tuck the edges so they don't show. As with any nondraining container, water minimally.

▶ Purple-stemmed trailing jade (*Senecio jacobsenii*) and other succulents grow in disks salvaged from a tractor plow. Pebbles conceal soil and root-balls.

◀ A repurposed minnow bucket contains graptopetalums and graptoverias.

▶▶ Each mint tin holds about a dozen small cuttings.

110

Fern's mint-tin minigarden

I now look at breath mint tins in a new way. Fern Richardson, author of *Small-Space Container Gardens*, plants succulents in the tins, creating minigardens that make great little hostess gifts and party favors.

Before planting a tin, Fern pokes a drain hole in the bottom using an awl or nail and hammer. To prevent the thin metal from becoming distorted by the impact, she inverts the box over a piece of wood. Fern hot-glues the hinges so the lid stays upright, fills the tin with cactus mix, and places marble-sized sempervivums, echeverias, or other cuttings atop the soil.

In a few weeks, they root and hold themselves in place. If a minigarden will sit on a surface potentially damaged by moisture, no drain hole may be best, but take care not to flood the box when watering the plants.

After seeing this idea on Fern's popular "Life on the Balcony" blog, I bought several brands of mints in order to have little boxes to plant. But any hinged container will do, as long as it's waterproof. Thrift stores sell lidded tins and boxes, often for less than a brand new box of mints.

COLLECTIBLE PLANTS IN COLLECTIBLE POTS

When it comes to premier succulents in gallery-quality pots presented with trophy-winning artistry, nothing can compare to what members of the Cactus and Succulent Society of America (CSSA) come up with. Founded in 1929 in Pasadena, the CSSA has eighty affiliated clubs and thousands of members worldwide. CSSA affiliates nationwide host shows and sales. These may be once or twice a year, depending on the club, and the public is welcome. Shows are primarily about collectible plants, and members present cacti and succulents that are rare, venerable, and in perfect condition.

In addition to amazing plants, you'll see pots that frame and present them perfectly—an art form called staging. This is different from dish gardens that combine several types of succulents in a way that suggests a floral arrangement or garden vignette. Staged pots hold only one plant, which is usually combined with rocks and topdressing. But if such elements or the container upstage the plant, they may be considered liabilities by show judges. Staging, when done well, doesn't call attention to itself, yet basic design principles do apply.

Among the many unusual plants on display at shows are those with nonsucculent leaves growing from the top of what appears to be a stack of sausages. These are caudiciforms—succulents that store water in bulbous roots. Preparing these roots in order to display them requires skill, patience, knowledge, and creativity. Roots need to be elevated above the soil level incrementally, a little more at each repotting. Skin that has never been exposed to air or sunlight has to be acclimated. Artistry enters in with deciding which roots to save and which to trim, selecting the right container, positioning the plant, and choosing and arranging rocks and topdressing.

Planting collectible succulents in collectible pots is an emerging trend. In the same amount of space, there's twice as much visual appeal. In addition to growers and nursery owners, vendors at CSSA shows and sales include artist-potters who make containers specifically to showcase cacti and succulents. These pots tend to be earth-toned or have a muted glaze (often blue-green) and are seldom shiny. Because one goal of staging is to present the plant as it might look in its natural habitat, pots may have a rustic texture or free-form shapes, or they may suggest fissures in rocks.

◀ In its natural habitat, this caudiciform is buried up to its crown (where the vining stems emerge). Its owner, CSSA member Keith Kitoi Taylor, creates his own pots—the better to present his award-winning collection of plants.

▼ An award-winning *Mammillaria canelensis* at the CSSA show at the Los Angeles Arboretum is perfect in the pot it occupies.

▲ A pot by Charles and Debbie Ball looks like it was scooped out of the earth, plant and all. Subtle repetitions include the color of the glaze with the blue-green of the 'Claudia' crassula, the plant's buds and the Grape Nuts–like topdressing; and the crackled glaze and the angles of the plant.

◀◀ Potter Don Hunt plants *Fockea edulis* (a caudiciform in the fig family) in one of his organic, free-form pots.

Two

HOW-TO PROJECTS THAT SHOWCASE SUCCULENTS

IT MAY SURPRISE you how easy it is to use succulents in bouquets, centerpieces, topiaries, and other floral and container creations. Florists employ rosette succulents as rose look-alikes that last vastly longer. Succulent cuttings, with their ability to seal themselves and survive without soil or water, are especially versatile. Professional garden designers, florists, and nursery owners tuck, wire, and pin succulents into their compositions—techniques that are especially useful when water and soil are messy or unnecessary. Perhaps the most astonishing technique is the moss-and-glue method used by garden designer Laura Eubanks, who laughingly says she can (and does) put succulents on anything.

For each project, you'll find lists of tools, materials, and plants. Substitutions are possible—indeed, desirable. It would be a shame if you didn't do a project that appeals to you because a certain succulent wasn't available. When you take your plant list to the nursery, include the Latin names. This is generally how plants are grouped, and if the nursery is out of, say, *Sempervivum arachnoideum*, chances are that similar plants in the genus *Sempervivum* will do.

Avoid handling the leaves. Once marred, fleshy leaves show damage forever. Hold rosettes and cuttings by their stems or, if there are none, the undersides of the leaves. Those with a powdery coating will show fingerprints, and the powder doesn't grow back. Aeonium foliage is especially sensitive to rough handling,

which shows the next day as dark creases. Graptopetalums, burro tail sedum, and many other succulents have leaves that detach easily. I wince when I hear that little *snap*.

However, you needn't be gentle with roots, which most succulents can do without for a long time—two weeks at least. At my potting workshops, I sometimes seize a pretty little potted echeveria and with a twist that makes a satisfying *crunch*, sever it from both its roots and nursery container. From the shocked faces in the audience, you'd think I'd beheaded a chicken. Without its roots, the rosette can be used in a bouquet or centerpiece. A week or even a month later, I'll pull the arrangement apart and plant the succulents, which are none the worse for the wear.

Most important, have fun. Enjoy these projects and do them with a friend or family member. I have a gal pal who requests every year on her birthday that we make something using succulents. She comes to my home with two other friends, and we chat while working at a table in the succulent sitting area. Although I'm the "expert," each brings her own style and taste to the project. The results invariably exceed everyone's expectations. You'll experience that, too.

See if succulents' ornamental potential doesn't surprise you. May these ideas serve as a springboard for your creativity and your own unique style.

◀◀ Designer Linda Estrin tucks a blooming cremnosedum amid *Graptoveria* 'Amethorum' in a container she made of hardware mesh.

Succulent Cake-Stand Centerpiece

DESIGN BY

Robyn Foreman, Vista, CA

EASY

LONG ASSOCIATED WITH layer cakes, plates atop pedestals are useful for showcasing another kind of eye candy: floral centerpieces. You might design this composition entirely with succulents, but bright flowers lend a festive touch. A cake-stand centerpiece of flowers alone is possible, too, but the addition of succulents adds interest and staying power. When the flowers are finished, you have the option of keeping the rest of the composition intact and replacing the flowers with fresh ones.

Because there's a wide range of floral material from which to choose, it can be daunting to know where to begin. You might start with a ruffled echeveria as a focal point and then select elements that repeat and contrast with it. Or take inspiration from flowers in season, or your event's theme and colors.

If the succulents you're using are rooted plants rather than cuttings, keep the root-balls if you like, but don't let them show. If they're not easily concealed, it's best to remove them. The succulents will still outlast the flowers and can be planted as cuttings later.

For a taller centerpiece, create a similar composition atop an elevated pedestal and add cascading string of pearls (*Senecio rowleyanus*) or rosary vine (*Ceropegia woodii*). For a looser bouquet that's equally pleasing, instead of using floral foam, insert flowers and greens into a wire or glass floral frog.

Caution: A floral knife's curved blade is useful for hooking around stems and slicing cleanly through them. However, if you are uncertain how to use this sharp tool, use clippers rather than risk injury.

◄◄ A centerpiece on a cake stand features echeverias and yellow ranunculus. Red in sempervivums on the upper right and on the tips of *Crassula* 'Campfire', upper left, repeats the red of the ruffled echeveria's leaf margins. Blue *Echeveria imbricata* rosettes on the lower right echo the shapes of the flowers and create a striking color contrast. Filler flowers include lime-green 'Kermit' mums and bright yellow *Craspedia globosa* (billy balls).

▲ When assembling your materials, get floral foam that absorbs water, not the kind used for dry arrangements.

MATERIALS

- clippers or floral knife (if you're proficient at using one)
- 12-inch-diameter glass cake stand
- several handfuls of green sheet moss (sold dry by the bag at nurseries and crafts stores)
- block of floral foam
- twelve to twenty cut flowers, 2 to 4 inches in diameter, with sturdy stems
- a dozen or so rosette and other succulents that have some shape or color in common with each other and with the flowers, as cuttings or in 2- to 4-inch nursery pots. Include a few that also offer pleasing contrasts such as fuzzy texture or pointed leaves.

▲ Damp moss surrounds a cube of water-retaining floral foam needed to keep cut flowers fresh.

▲ After sliding succulents out of their nursery pots and removing the soil, arrange them on the plate, starting with the largest.

1. Soak the floral foam in water until saturated, slice it into a cube, and position it off center on the plate.

2. Submerge the moss, squeeze it to get rid of excess moisture, and arrange it around the foam.

3. Insert flower stems into the top and sides of the foam so its edges and outward-facing sides are covered. Petals should touch or overlap.

4. Slide succulents from their nursery pots and shake excess soil from the roots (or remove them).

5. Arrange the succulents on the plate, starting with the largest. Fill in with smaller succulents and additional floral material.

6. Aim for an arrangement shaped like an inverted bowl. Rosette succulents along the edge should face outward so the composition looks good from all sides. If a rosette or cutting is top-heavy, support it with moss or push its stem into the foam.

7. If blooms are vivid, repeat their color on the opposite side of the arrangement for continuity and balance. Ideally use smaller flowers that are the same color but a different size or shape. Instead of grouping, dot them.

8. If flowers or greens not inserted in the floral foam are at risk of wilting, insert their stems into thumb-sized pieces of soaked foam cut from the unused portion of the block.

◄ Yellow ranunculus that echoes the concentricity of the echeveria rosettes joins the button mums held in place by floral foam.

CARE

Moisture in the moss and foam will likely be enough to keep the flowers fresh for a week, possibly longer. Even so, check after several days. If need be, add water to the plate, and the foam will absorb it.

◀ The final arrangement is higher in the middle, lower around the edges. Note how designer Robyn Foreman contrasted and repeated shapes, textures, and colors.

Succulent Squares

DESIGN BY

Linda Estrin, Linda Estrin Garden Design, Oak Park, CA

EASY

LOS ANGELES–AREA GARDEN DESIGNER and succulent floral artist Linda Estrin celebrates the symmetry of succulents by planting them in square containers. Because uniformity is important in a geometric composition, she often selects similar-looking sempervivum or echeveria rosettes. Linda plants these in a tic-tac-toe pattern, then fills the rest of the container with a finer-leaved succulent that offers elements of contrast and repetition. She "signs" her compositions by adding a third type of succulent that complements aspects of the others, which she positions at one corner of the center rosette. This last off-center element lends a touch of whimsy.

Square containers are sold in larger garden centers and nurseries, and online (enter "square flower pot" into a search engine). They should be just 3 inches deep or less; anything deeper will be out of scale with muffin-sized echeverias and sempervivums. (A better choice for a cube-shaped pot is a solo succulent with roots that will fill it halfway or more—perhaps an aloe or agave.)

Estrin makes her own containers, including heart-shaped ones, using ½-inch wire mesh (also known as hardware cloth or hardware mesh) sold at home improvement stores. Drawing on her sewing experience, she cuts and folds the mesh, then wires the corners together. To hold in soil and add a decorative element, she lines the box with nonwoven fabric, which comes in assorted colors. If the finished composition is a gift, she may wrap the sides with ribbon.

◀◀ One of many possible square compositions incorporates succulents with reddish leaves: *Sempervivum* 'Ohioan', *Cremnosedum* 'Little Gem' in bud, and *Crassula* 'Campfire'.

◀ Possible plants for a square composition are spiky *Echeveria purpusorum* and, for contrast, finer-textured *Monanthes muralis*. Red-leaved peperomia might lend color and contrast.

MATERIALS

- square container, 8 inches wide by 2 inches deep
- chopstick
- long-handled tweezers
- five red-and-green sempervivum or echeveria rosettes in 3-inch nursery pots
- four 3-inch pots of a finer-leaved succulent that repeats or contrasts with colors found in the larger rosettes
- potting soil

▲ Linda folds nonwoven fabric so it fits inside the wire box, then staples it in place. A square of window screen helps stabilize the container without impeding drainage.

▲ Pack soil ½ inch deep.

◀ Add plants in a tic-tac-toe pattern, then fill gaps with potting soil.

1. If the soil is dry and crumbly, moisten it so it holds together.

2. Pack soil into the bottom of the container, pressing it into corners, to a depth of ½ inch.

3. Select four uniform rosettes for the corners, plus a fifth (which might be slightly different from the rest, not necessarily the largest) to go in the center.

4. Slide the rosettes from their pots. Remove enough soil from the bottom of the root-balls so that lower leaves are flush with the rim of the container.

5. Place the rosettes in the container, one at each corner and one in the middle.

6. Remove finer-leaved succulents from their pots and use to fill the remaining openings on each of the four sides.

7. Using the blunt end of a chopstick, push additional soil into gaps between the plants.

8. Remove any soil that has fallen into the rosettes with long-handled tweezers or a dry paintbrush.

9. Lightly spray the composition with water to clean the leaves and settle the roots.

CARE

Give bright light but not direct sun so plants keep their color but don't sunburn. Sempervivums indicate that they are not getting enough light if they turn from red to green and their lower leaves curl downward. These succulents are especially prone to root rot, so water sparingly once every two weeks or so. If you should happen to lose a rosette, pull it out and replace it.

▶ Four designs illustrate how diverse square compositions can be.

Additional square-pot plant combos

Aeonium 'Kiwi' with *Sedum* 'Tricolor' as filler

Agave lophantha 'Quadricolor' with *Portulacaria afra* 'Variegata', *Sedum* 'Angelina', or *Sedum makinoi* 'Ogon' as filler

Aloe nobilis with *Sedum rubrotinctum* 'Pork and Beans' as filler

Aloe 'Pink Blush' with peperomia as filler

Echeveria imbricata with *Sedum* 'Dragon's Blood', *Sedum* 'Blue Spruce', or *Crassula* 'Baby's Necklace' as filler

Echeveria 'Perle von Nurnberg' with *Sedum rubrotinctum* 'Aurora' as filler

Mammillarias with astrophytums as filler

Sempervivum arachnoideum with *Sedum anglicum* or *Senecio rowleyanus* as filler

Living Picture Vertical Garden

DESIGN BY

Emma Alpaugh and Debra Lee Baldwin

EASY

ONE OR MORE LIVING pictures may be just the ticket if an important view—such as your kitchen window's—is of a blank fence or wall, or if you'd like to add interest to a breezeway, loggia, or garden gate. Robin Stockwell, owner of Succulent Gardens nursery near San Francisco, is renowned for such living murals, large and small. The projects shown here use framed planter boxes Stockwell innovated and sells.

The concept is simple: you'll need a shallow, waterproof box that holds soil, with its open side (front) covered with ½-inch wire mesh, sold by the roll at home improvement stores. Fill the box by pushing soil through the mesh. Arrange succulent rosettes atop the mesh or tuck stem cuttings through it into the soil. After a few weeks, numerous threadlike roots will have emerged from the base of each rosette. As roots

◀◀ Two completed living pictures, side by side, suggest the variety possible; Emma's has blue and pink echeverias and kalanchoe cuttings in bloom; mine features red 'Campfire' crassula. Both compositions also incorporate marble-sized echeveria and sempervivum rosettes.

seek soil they'll wrap around the mesh and hold the plants firmly in place. When this has happened, you can hang the picture. Or display it flat, set it atop an outdoor shelf or ledge, or prop it upright on a table.

Since gravity can cause soil to slump, and the greater the volume the greater the weight, the maximum size a box can be is 18 × 24 inches. Larger vertical gardens are best created in premade plastic containers that have rows of individual plantable cells. These allow water to percolate downward and are angled so soil doesn't fall out. Another option is to align or arrange several planted frames to create the look of a larger one.

Sempervivums, small echeverias (such as *Echeveria minima* and *Echeveria elegans*), aeoniums (such as 'Kiwi' or *Aeonium haworthii*), and most stonecrops stay small and won't outgrow the arrangement. Robin suggests contrasting *Sempervivum arachnoideum* with red-tipped *Sempervivum calcareum*, and lavender-pink *Echeveria*

'Perle von Nurnberg' with blue *Echeveria secunda*. A focal point, such as a larger aeonium or echeveria rosette, can be pulled out and replaced later if it outgrows the composition. If you use cuttings in bloom, each needs a pair of leaves attached in order to root.

Lay out your design first on a flat surface or simply create it, as we did, as you go along. It might be free-form or striped, have a geometric pattern, or depict a star, butterfly, or even someone's initial. Also pleasing is an S-shaped river of plants surrounded by those of a contrasting color. Once you've assembled and prepped the plants and filled the frame with soil, creating a composition goes quickly—those shown here took about ten minutes each.

MATERIALS

- premade frame from Succulent Gardens (or make your own; see pages 136–137)
- potting soil
- fork
- chopstick
- enough small succulent rosettes or cuttings to cover and conceal the mesh (the 12 × 6 frames shown here used an average of sixty-eight cuttings each, varying in size from ½ inch to 2½ inches in diameter)

◀ Emma's blue-purple-yellow composition used approximately sixty rosettes or cuttings:

- five *Echeveria* 'Perle von Nurnberg' rosettes (from 1 to 2½ inches in diameter)
- ten *Echeveria minima* rosettes (from ½ inch to 2½ inches)
- twelve graptosedum cuttings
- fifteen sempervivum rosettes (averaging ½ inch)
- eighteen kalanchoe cuttings (yellow-flowered supermarket kalanchoes and purple *Kalanchoe pumila*)

◀ My red-blue-green composition used approximately seventy-five rosettes or cuttings:

- five *Aeonium* 'Kiwi' cuttings (from 1 to 2 inches)
- six *Crassula caput-minima* cuttings (averaging 1½ inches)
- twelve *Crassula* 'Campfire' cuttings (from 1 to 2 inches)
- twenty *Sempervivum arachnoideum* rosettes (between ½ and 1 inch)
- thirty-two *Echeveria minima* rosettes (between ½ and 1 inch)

1. First, prepare the plants. Pull sempervivum offsets away from the mother plant and trim their umbilical-cord-like roots to just below the bottom leaves. Take cuttings of small echeverias, aeoniums, kalanchoes, and jade, leaving about ¼ inch of stem below the lowest leaves. Peel away any dry, papery leaves at the base of the rosettes. Set rosettes and cuttings aside for a day or two to let raw tissue heal.

2. If the frame would look best varnished or painted, do so before planting it. The same goes for attaching screw eyes and picture-frame wire

▲ Possible succulents for a living picture include sempervivums, echeverias, kalanchoes (in bloom), sedums, and aeoniums. This is just a sampling; many more kinds will work.

◀◀ The plantable frame isn't watertight—a good thing, because you don't want water to pool inside it.

to the back. Adding these to top and bottom will enable you to rotate the frame for even light exposure.

3. Fill the box with potting soil by rubbing it through the screen with your fingertips. Don't press too hard or you may dislodge the screen. Tap the box on the work surface to settle the soil, then add more to the level of the wire mesh. Taking care not to pull the screen out of the frame, use a fork to raise the mesh slightly as you push additional soil through. Optionally, use the blunt end of a chopstick to tamp the soil.

4. As you arrange rosettes atop the mesh, don't focus on filling squares. Rather, consider how the plants might be arrayed in a pleasing way. Leaves should barely touch each other. You're done when no mesh shows. Evaluate the results and rearrange the plants until you're satisfied.

5. After planting, keep the container flat, in bright shade. It's OK if succulents shrivel a bit before roots form. Once they're able to take up water, they'll be fine.

6. Wait a week, then lift one of the rosettes to see if it has roots. If not, wait another week and check again. When roots have formed, water the box just enough to moisten the soil. By the next day, plants will have plumped and regained their sheen.

7. When gentle tugging does not dislodge the plants, you can hang the living picture. Moisture will seep from the box and collect behind and below it, so protect any surfaces not waterproof. Display it in an area with good air circulation, with morning sun or dappled shade.

▲ After pushing potting mix though the screen and tapping the frame on the table to settle it, Emma uses a fork to lift the mesh slightly so additional soil can go underneath. Soil should be as close to the mesh as possible (without covering it) so plants root readily.

▲ When inserting stem cuttings, use the pointed end of the chopstick to poke holes in the soil.

▲ Emma's completed composition includes lavender and yellow kalanchoe flowers.

CARE

Lay the box flat to water it. Do so lightly when the soil is nearly dry—about once a week in summer, once a month in winter. Don't overwater.

Make your own frame or repurpose a used picture frame

If you're handy, you can make your own plantable frame. Per Robin Stockwell, for one that is 12 inches square, you'll need four 12-inch lengths of 2 × 2 redwood or cedar, mitered 45 degrees at the corners. Create a groove along the inside, $^3/_8$ inch below the face and parallel to it. This ¼-inch-deep channel, which is the width of a saw blade ($^1/_{16}$ inch), holds an 11½-inch square of ½-inch screen (hardware mesh). A second groove parallel to the back holds the backing, which can be a piece of light-weight plastic or a $^3/_8$-inch-thick, 12 × 12 piece of water-resistant (marine) plywood or backer board (used in shower stalls). Assemble the pieces with a staple gun or rustproof nails.

For a soilless option, scour thrift stores for pictures that in themselves are not worth having but have a wood frame you like. It should be deep enough to hold a layer of moss that's at least 1 inch thick. Cut hardware mesh and a piece of plywood the same dimensions as the frame. Using a staple gun, attach the mesh to

the back of the frame. Create a dense pillow of moss by sandwiching as much as possible between mesh and plywood. (We used a 6-quart bag of dry green moss for an 8 × 10 pillow, 1½ inches deep.) Staple, nail, or screw the plywood to the frame. Assemble and prep your cuttings, leaving about ½ inch of stem, and then use a chopstick or knitting needle to make holes in the moss as you plant it. Follow the same care instructions as for the living picture, aiming to keep the moss barely moist.

You can also attach succulent rosettes directly onto a picture (or onto a plywood backing that shows through the frame) using the moss-and-glue method described in the pumpkin project later in this section. Or replace the picture with one you do like, then glue moss and succulents around the frame instead of inside it. Everything should handle being spritzed several times a week.

◀◀ Make your own plantable frame with redwood or cedar 2 × 2s, wire mesh, and some kind of backing (this one has a piece of lightweight plastic).

◀ A used picture frame can be repurposed as a living picture. I painted this thrift store frame green to match my outdoor furniture and antiqued it with bronze.

Low-Light
Dish Garden

DESIGN BY
Jon Hawley, Chicweed, Solana Beach, CA

EASY

AS LIGHT LOVERS, most succulents prefer to be grown outdoors in full sun or, at a minimum, in bright shade. But certain succulents do fine in low-light conditions, making them good choices for indoor arrangements or shady outdoor areas. These plants also look good with each other and offer a variety of shapes and textures.

Jon Hawley's low-light dish garden combines snake plants (*Sansevieria trifasciata*) with super-market kalanchoes (*Kalanchoe blossfeldiana*),

◀ Jon's dish garden has repetitions of pale greens, dark greens, light yellows, points, stripes, and zigzags. Coral and rose kalanchoe blooms provide contrast.

variegated aloes, and jewel-like haworthias. The sansevierias are important for height, so they dictate the rest of the composition's plants, which repeat their characteristics or contrast with them. Because the leaves of supermarket kalanchoes are less important from a design standpoint than the blooms, Jon made sure the flowers show.

The arrangement includes an area of sand in the foreground. Such negative space creates the illusion of distance and draws the viewer in. Plant material gets gradually higher toward the back. "I like to suggest that you're going from the seashore to the mountains," Jon says.

Succulents for low-light situations

For the most part, shade succulents are in hues of green and yellow. Supermarket kalanchoes and calandivas (both are types of *Kalanchoe blossfeldiana*) are useful for offering a wider range of colors for the shade-plant palette. These succulents have been hybridized extensively to be the ultimate low-maintenance, low-water houseplants and to produce abundant flower clusters in every warm hue. Purchase them in bud for six weeks of nonstop floral color. Supermarket kalanchoes are rebloomers in the garden but may not flower again indoors unless grown near a sunny window.

Snake plants (sansevierias) are wonderful indoor plants, too, with a tolerance for neglect as well as dim light. All have tapered and pointed leaves. Numerous kinds range from tall and cylindrical to short and wedge shaped, and from pale to dark green or variegated.

Other low-light options include crested succulents, and yellow- or cream-striped versions of sun-loving succulents. Among these are variegates of *Aloe nobilis*, *Agave attenuata*, and *Cotyledon tomentosa*.

FOR HEIGHT:

Aeonium species (green or variegated; black aeoniums need full sun)
Kalanchoe blossfeldiana hybrids
Sansevieria cylindrica
Sansevieria trifasciata 'Variegata'

SMALL-TO-MEDIUM FILLERS:

crested succulents
Gasteria species
Hatiora salicornioides (dancing bones cactus)
Haworthia species
Kalanchoe blossfeldiana hybrids
Peperomia species
Sansevieria cultivars with triangular leaves
Sedum makinoi 'Ogon'

CASCADERS:

Ceropegia woodii (rosary vine)
Hoya species (wax plant)
Rhipsalis species (mistletoe cactus)
Senecio rowleyanus (string of pearls)

▲ Succulents for a low-light arrangement include supermarket kalanchoes, snake plants, dwarf and variegated aloes, and haworthias.

MATERIALS

- 2- to 3-inch-deep, 12-inch-diameter container
- potting soil
- handful of small stones
- coarse white sand (not beach sand, which contains salts) for topdressing
- plastic spoon
- chopstick
- two similarly colored supermarket kalanchoes (*Kalanchoe blossfeldiana*), one larger than the other (one in a 4-inch pot, one in a 2-inch pot)
- two snake plants in 4-inch pots: one tall (*Sansevieria trifasciata* 'Laurentii') and one medium with yellow-variegated, triangular leaves (*Sansevieria trifasciata* 'Laurentii', dwarf form; or *Sansevieria* 'Golden Hahnii')
- 4-inch pot of a variegated (pale- and dark-green) dwarf aloe with offsets (such as 'Lizard Lips' or 'Doran Black')
- 3-inch pot of *Aloe nobilis* 'Variegata'
- 3-inch pot of crested *Euphorbia flanaganii*
- 2-inch pot of *Hatiora salicornioides* (dancing bones cactus)
- three 2-inch pots of assorted haworthias, such as *Haworthia turgida*, *Haworthia cooperi*, and *Haworthia retusa*

1. Fill the container with moist potting soil.

2. Add the large supermarket kalanchoe first, placing it in the back alongside the rim.

3. Add the snake plants to the back third of the container, flanking the kalanchoe.

4. Position the dwarf aloe cluster in front of the kalanchoe and between the snake plants, so everything frames the flowers.

5. Add the variegated gold tooth aloe in front of the taller of the two sansevierias.

6. Leaving the hatiora for last, plant the remaining succulents in a curve that repeats the container's, leaving several inches for the "beach." The second, smaller kalanchoe goes left of center.

7. Spread open the hatiora's root-ball and use the plant to form a fringe that extends from the aloe cluster to the edge of the pot.

8. Use the chopstick to push soil against the plant roots and settle them.

9. Use the plastic spoon to add sand, covering any bare dirt. Strew gravel and rocks on the sand.

10. Water the arrangement lightly, taking care not to displace the sand.

▶ In a composition intended to be viewed mainly from one side, tall plants go in back, shorter in front.

▲ Succulents are shallow rooted, so a round, shallow container is appropriate as well as attractive.

▲ As Jon holds a cluster of dwarf aloes upright with one hand, he pushes soil against their roots with the other. His favorite tool is a chopstick; here, he's using its blunt end.

CARE

Indoors or out, give your low-light arrangement bright light but not direct sun, lest leaves burn. If need be in order to protect wood or other porous surfaces, place the pot on a saucer, but avoid letting the container sit in water more than an hour or two. Give plants good air circulation and check occasionally for mealybugs and other indoor-plant pests.

Hanging Basket
of Mixed Succulents

DESIGN BY

Melissa Teisl, Chicweed, Solana Beach, CA

MODERATELY EASY

IF YOU GARDEN on a deck, patio, or balcony but are running out of room, the answer might be right in front of you: empty air space. A hanging basket of succulents can contain a lavish assortment that suggests a garden bed. Best of all, succulents won't wilt, as most plants do, if their airy container dries out. Nor do succulents require frequent and inconvenient soakings.

A hanging basket needs three heavy-gauge chains securely attached to the rim, equidistant from each other and all the same length. Make sure the chains are strong enough that the rings will not separate from the weight of wet soil and plants. Secure the hook that holds the chains to

◀ Sturdy premade baskets are inexpensive at garden centers and nurseries, and are also sold online. This one is chock full, but you could use fewer plants.

a ceiling stud or overhead beam. A fishing swivel between the ceiling hook and the loop above the chains makes it possible to turn the basket without having to detach and rehang it. (The swivel's conventional use is to keep the line from twisting as a fish is reeled in.)

You might base your plant selection on a color scheme, such as warm reds, oranges, and purples; or cool blues, purples, and greens. Or simply choose an assortment of succulents that appeal to you. A ruffled echeveria that combines several colors can serve to bridge disparate elements. A dozen succulents in 4- and 6-inch pots, with a variety of forms and textures, will give you plenty to play with. Have handy two basketfuls of potting soil. As with the plant material, you'll need more than you think.

◀ The basket's liner holds in soil and moisture. The soft brush is for cleaning spilled dirt from leaves, the chopstick for pushing soil around roots and settling them, and the plastic spoon for adding soil to gaps.

▼ An assortment of succulents, in varying sizes and textures, includes focal points, fillers, and cascaders. Melissa used all except the graptoveria, upper left, and the 'Fish Hooks' senecio (*Senecio radicans*) next to it.

▲ A bucket is useful for catching soil that falls off of root-balls.

MATERIALS
- 12-inch-diameter lined basket, with chains attached
- plastic spoon
- chopstick
- soft artist's brush
- potting soil (approximately ¼ cubic foot)
- 8-inch pot of ruffled echeveria
- 6-inch pot of *Kalanchoe luciae* (paddle plant)
- 6-inch pot of *Portulacaria afra* (elephant's food)
- 4-inch pots, one of each:
- *Echeveria imbricata* (blue rose echeveria)
- *Aloe brevifolia* (short-leaf aloe)
- *Aeonium* 'Kiwi'
- *Cotyledon tomentosa* (kitten paws)
- *Sedum nussbaumerianum* (coppertone stone-crop)
- *Sedum* 'Angelina'
- *Sedum burrito* (burro tail stonecrop)
- *Cremnosedum* 'Little Gem'

▲ Start just off center with high, large, or dramatic elements. Surround with midsize succulents.

1. Using the pointed end of the chopstick, poke a hole in the liner for drainage. Fill the basket three-quarters full of soil.

2. Start with the largest plants and situate them off center. You'll build the rest of the composition around them.

3. Working from largest to smallest, nestle additional plants around the large ones. Evaluate the distribution and balance of colors as you go.

4. If a potted succulent consists of multiple rooted stems (often the case with elephant's food and kitten paws), hold the root-ball together lest the stems flop apart.

▲ It's surprising how many plants you can stuff into a 12-inch-diameter basket. As they grow over the edge, the arrangement will become looser and airier. You could also use cuttings instead of rooted plants; fewer plants (they'll fill in over time); or one kind of cascading succulent only.

5. Rotate the faces of rosette succulents toward the basket's edge.

6. Add trailing or ground-cover succulents (such as *Sedum* 'Angelina' and *Sedum burrito*) last, just inside the rim. It may seem there's no room for these, but if you spread open their root-balls, you can tuck the plants around the base of a larger plant like a collar. Handle the *Sedum burrito* gingerly, because its beadlike leaves come off easily.

7. Tuck in plants and push soil under large leaves with the blunt end of the chopstick. Use the plastic spoon to add soil where your fingers can't reach. Gently brush spilled soil off leaves with a soft paintbrush.

Trailing succulents

Most stem succulents will become pendant over time as they seek soil in which to root. These specifically vining types prefer bright light rather than shade:

Aporocactus flagelliformis (rat-tail cactus)
Crassula, stacked varieties
Graptopetalum paraguayense (ghost plant)
Ice plants
Othonna capensis
Portulacaria afra 'Minima' (prostrate
    elephant's food)
Portulacaria afra 'Variegata' (variegated
    elephant's food)
Schlumbergera (Christmas cactus)
Sedums (stonecrops)
Senecio kleiniiformis (spear head)
Senecio radicans 'Fish Hooks'
    ('Fish Hooks' senecio)

▲ Another view of the completed basket, several weeks later. A similar composition might be done in a pot the same size.

CARE

A plastic-lined hanging basket needs watering on average every other week—more frequently in summer, less in winter. Protect the composition from wind, harsh sun, freezing temperatures, and excessive rainfall. To balance light exposure, rotate the basket 180 degrees every week or two.

Succulent-Topped Pumpkins

DESIGN BY

Laura Eubanks, Design for Serenity, San Diego

MODERATELY EASY

GARDEN DESIGNER Laura Eubanks was wearing earrings decorated with itty-bitty sedum rosettes when we met. Several months later, I saw her at a garden show, where she displayed a 3-foot-long wire alligator she had covered with small succulents. Children crouched in front of "Roberto," fascinated. Laura's technique is to use spray glue to attach sphagnum moss to a surface, such as a seashell, and then a hot-glue gun to attach succulent rosettes to the moss. Surprisingly, the hot glue doesn't harm the plants.

Laura's succulent-topped pumpkins, adorned also with berries and seedpods, make great centerpieces, hostess gifts, and entryway decorations. Note that the succulents are planted *atop* the pumpkin, not in it. Pumpkins can be as small as a bagel or so large you can barely lift them. I like 'Cinderella' pumpkins, which are deeply grooved with bowl-shaped tops, but smaller pumpkins are also appealing and look

good grouped or aligned atop a dining table.

You might assume such designs are ephemeral, like floral arrangements. After all, the succulents aren't planted . . . or are they? Actually, they are. Laura's method takes advantage of the way succulent cuttings conserve water in their leaves and stay fresh while their stems send forth hairlike roots. Amazingly, the cuttings root right through the glue, into the moss. The only care such compositions require is occasional misting to moisten the moss. Without soil, the plants don't grow much, which is what you want. Growth deconstructs any tight arrangement. With proper care, it will last as long as the pumpkin does. Laura kept one looking good for nine months.

I prefer not to use a hot-glue gun because of the danger of burns. However, if you're proficient with one, it can be a time saver. Never touch the glue when hot. Hold tiny rosettes with long-handled tweezers when applying it; spread it with a popsicle stick or apply the glue to the moss and then press the rosettes into it. Keep ice water handy so you can instantly cool hot glue that accidentally comes into contact with your skin. More tips can be found online by typing "glue gun safety" into a search engine.

Someday Laura's moss-and-glue method might revolutionize the way floral-bedecked parade floats are made. Those of Pasadena's Tournament of Roses parade, which are required to be covered in floral material, traditionally use mums and other ephemeral blooms kept fresh for about a week in tiny vials. Succulents, which come in as many colors as flowers, last far longer yet need no water and could prove to be less labor intensive and more cost effective in other ways as well.

◀◀ Larger cuttings and dried seedpods are in the center, with smaller cuttings and embellishments around the edge.

▼ Tools include two kinds of craft glue and clippers for taking cuttings. The seedpods were collected by Laura on walks through her neighborhood.

MATERIALS

- clean 8- to 12-inch-diameter pumpkin with a concave top without a stem or with the stem removed
- sphagnum moss (sold by the bag at craft stores)
- spray adhesive, such as Elmer's Craft Bond
- clear gel glue, such as Aleene's, or a hot-glue gun
- woody seedpods (such as eucalyptus and magnolia), acorns, rose hips, or nuts in the shell
- a few clusters of red-orange berries, such as pyracantha, red pepper (*Schinus molle*), or cotoneaster
- a cheerful assortment of small succulents—the more colors and textures the merrier
- scissors

The larger of the two pumpkins has approximately fifty 1- to 3-inch rosettes or cuttings of these succulents:

- *Aeonium* 'Kiwi'
- *Crassula* 'Campfire'
- *Echeveria minima*
- *Graptosedum* 'California Sunset'
- *Haworthia attenuata* (zebra plant)
- *Kalanchoe tomentosa* (panda plant)
- *Sedum* 'Angelina'
- *Sedum* 'Blue Spruce'
- *Sedum* 'Cape Blanco'
- *Sedum burrito* (burro tail)
- *Sedum rubrotinctum* 'Pork and Beans'

▼ A bed of moss gives succulent cuttings a medium in which to root.

1. Coat the pumpkin's bowl-shaped top with spray glue.

2. Press dry moss onto the glue to form a ½-inch-thick bed.

3. Using clear craft glue or hot glue to hold them in place, add the succulent rosettes atop the moss, beginning with the largest (just off center) and adding successively smaller ones as you work outward. Intermingle them with the dried materials.

▲ Pumpkins topped with succulents make eye-catching autumn centerpieces.

4. Surround the center rosettes with daintier succulents, such as sedums.

5. As you add more cuttings and dry items, aim for good balance and variety. You want an abundant look with no moss showing, plus an eclectic mix of colors and textures.

6. Using scissors, trim excess moss.

CARE

Once or twice a week (more frequently if humidity is low), spritz the arrangement with water to refresh the leaves and moss, and to keep fine roots from desiccating. Do not, however, let water pool in the top of the pumpkin. Succulents will retain their bright colors and tight forms for up to a week indoors in low light but then will need at least several hours of bright light daily to keep from reverting to green or stretching. A cool, dry location is best. If the pumpkin sits on an impermeable, damp surface, like concrete, it will soon soften, so place it atop a trivet or something that allows air to circulate (even corrugated cardboard will do). Also protect the pumpkin from frost. To salvage the succulents, take cuttings; set the entire pumpkin in the garden; or slice off the top and plant it.

Glue-only ideas

It's possible to glue succulents to any number of objects with or without first adding a layer of moss for the plants to root into. If kept out of direct sun, the following glue-only ideas will stay fresh for several weeks or more.

HAIR ORNAMENTS Wear little "flowers" in your hair by gluing tiny sedum rosettes to a barrette, tiara, wreath, plastic headband, comb, or clip.

PACKAGE TOPPER Tie dried twigs with raffia, glue succulents in the center, and use instead of a bow. Wrap the package with an organic-looking paper in soft earth tones that complement the plants' muted hues.

PARTY FAVORS Glue dainty rosettes to napkin rings that guests can take home as mementos.

HOLIDAY ORNAMENTS Top pinecones with tiny rosette succulents and add little bells, glass balls, or toys.

FESTIVE PET COLLAR Glue succulent rosettes to your dog's or kitty's collar so your pet will be dressed appropriately for your garden event.

▲ Laura Eubanks glued tiny sedum rosettes and the beadlike leaves of string of pearls (senecio) to a hair clip.

Succulent
Topiary Sphere

DESIGN BY

Debra Lee Baldwin

ADVANCED

SUCCULENTS LOOK TERRIFIC planted in traditional topiary shapes, and ball-shaped cobweb house-leeks *(Sempervivum arachnoideum)* are especially appealing for spheres. Moreover, cobweb house-leek "chicks" are attached to the colony via stems that come out cleanly and easily. You can thread these stems, which resemble mouse tails, beneath the topiary form's twigs or wires and pull tight to anchor the rosettes in place.

For the project shown here, I obtained small cobweb houseleeks from a nursery that let me harvest them from half-gallon containers of mature plants (which looked none the worse afterward). For color and texture interest, I added burgundy red sempervivums with pointed tips. Because the white-webbed houseleeks have

◀ Tail-like stems of cobweb houseleeks extend from the partially completed topiary.

reddish outer leaves, they serve as a bridge between the dark red rosettes and a cream-colored urn that completes the composition.

A sphere should be in proportion to whatever it sits on, so shop for both topiary form and container at the same time, or take your vase, urn, or pot with you when selecting an orb to plant. Keep in mind that the sphere will gain about 2 inches in diameter when planted.

I used a topiary form made of twigs, which I filled with moist moss and then glued the semps to. Possible adhesives include inexpensive craft glue (which is water soluble, so don't soak the sphere until the rosettes have rooted through the glue—wait several weeks); a nonsoluble but comparatively costly glue designed for fabric projects; or if you're proficient at using one, a glue gun. Hot glue has the advantages that it sticks to damp moss, isn't water soluble, and adheres instantly so there's no concern about gravity causing rosettes to fall off. U-shaped floral pins are useful for attaching the rosettes, too, but the pins poke holes in the plants and rust over time.

My topiary form and plaster urn came from a floral supply house, the glue and moss from a craft store. Starting with a moss orb would save you a step, but make sure it's solid moss and not a skin of moss over Styrofoam. I used hens-and-chicks because they don't get leggy, but any small rosette succulents—including echeverias, stacked crassulas, or even dwarf aloes—would work.

This project has spin-off potential as well. You might use the same method to create a succulent wreath or, for that matter, to plant any moss-filled form. Hanging the orb is another option, but there are benefits to having it sit atop a vase or urn: you needn't cover the bottom of the sphere, it's easier to plant and to water, and it's not as vulnerable to the elements. If you do decide to hang the sphere, add a sturdy hook to the top, suspend the ball as you plant it (in order to access the bottom), and use craft glue plus U-shaped floral pins (or hot glue) to secure the lowest rosettes.

▼ The twig ball for a succulent topiary sphere should be in proportion to the container. No potting soil is needed; the plants will grow in moss.

MATERIALS

- 6-inch-diameter twig ball
- 12-quart bag of green moss
- a few drops of household bleach (to prevent mold)
- chopstick
- bottle of craft glue or a hot-glue gun
- garden clippers or scissors
- container to support the planted ball (my urn is 7 inches wide by 7½ inches high)
- stones for ballast
- a hundred or so *Sempervivum arachnoideum* rosettes ranging in size from peas to ping-pong balls
- thirty red-hued sempervivum rosettes (I used 'Devil's Food', but the variety doesn't matter)

OPTIONAL:

- twenty or so U-shaped floral pins

1. Soak the moss in water to which a few drops of household bleach have been added. Moist moss is easier to work with and packs better. Squeeze out excess water.

2. Stuff the ball with as much moss as it'll hold, and also tuck moss into gaps between twigs. The goal is to provide a medium the plants will root into and that has a core that retains moisture.

3. Place the moss-stuffed ball in the sun to dry for a day or two. If you'll be using a water-soluble glue, the surface shouldn't be damp except at the bottom of the sphere.

4. Prep the rosettes. Pull chicks apart from hens, remove any soil, and peel away lowest leaves if dry or downward curving. Keep any umbilical-cord-like stems.

5. Place stones in the urn to offset the weight of the sphere, and set the sphere atop the urn.

◀ The twig ball, packed tightly with moss, is ready for planting.

6. Coat the underside of each rosette with glue, then press it onto the orb, beginning at the bottom and working upward. If you accidentally glue the sphere to the urn's rim, let the glue dry, sever it with a knife, and peel it off.

7. As you glue cobweb houseleeks, use the chopstick to push their tails under or around the form's twigs or wires to secure the plants (not necessary if you're using hot glue).

8. Intersperse the cobweb houseleeks with other sempervivums (or tiny echeverias) that provide contrasting color and texture. If gravity causes these to fall off, tuck them above or between houseleeks, secure with U-shaped floral pins, or add glue to the ball's surface and let dry to a tacky consistency before adding the rosette. It's OK to hold the rosettes in place until the glue sets, but do so gently lest you damage the leaves.

9. Save the littlest rosettes for last and use to fill small gaps. But don't be overly concerned about concealing every bit of the ball; it's fine if some moss and twigs show.

10. Let the glue dry overnight, then trim any cobweb houseleek tails that are visible.

CARE

Keep the planted sphere out of full, hot sun for several weeks, rotating it every few days for even exposure. If humidity is low and temperatures high, mist the topiary daily to keep leaves hydrated, but don't soak the moss lest water dissolve the glue that holds rosettes in place. (This is not a concern if you used a glue gun.) In two weeks to a month, roots will have grown from the base of each rosette through the glue,

▲ Before pressing each rosette onto the form, I coated the underside with tacky craft glue.

▶▶ An orb planted with sempervivum rosettes makes a conversation-starting enhancement for a balcony, patio, or other garden sitting area.

around the twigs, and into the moss. You can then introduce the sphere to stronger sunlight, adding a half hour each day, up to an optimal three hours daily. Water the topiary once a week or so, depending on the weather. The ball should feel heavy; if it's lightweight, pour water on the top until the bottom drips. Discard water that collects in the urn. As the sempervivums produce offsets, the topiary will look even fuller. To fill gaps, pull an offset loose (or snip it off) and insert where needed.

Special-Occasion Succulent Bouquet

DESIGN BY

Robyn Foreman, Vista, CA

ADVANCED

A BOUQUET THAT includes succulent rosettes offers both sentiment and mementos. After the flowers have faded, you can remove the succulents and plant them in a pot or in the garden, where they'll serve as living reminders of the occasion. They may even produce offspring before the bride and groom do! Include the same type of succulents in the event's table centerpieces, corsages, boutonnieres, and hair ornaments, so friends and family will have remembrance plants for their own gardens, too.

You might use a particularly lovely echeveria as your signature succulent in special-occasion bouquets now and for years to come. Think of it—a bride could keep the same plant going long enough for its descendants to be in her own daughter's wedding bouquet.

Although it's possible to create this without a bouquet holder, if the arrangement will need to be carried for any length of time, a holder is a good idea. It's a disk of floral foam enclosed in a plastic cage that is attached to a handle by which the bouquet can be held. You also may want a frill that fits beneath the bouquet and hides the container. Such items are inexpensive and available at floral suppliers, many crafts stores, and online.

Instead of tossing this bouquet after the wedding and potentially damaging the succulents, a bride should have a smaller, lightweight "tossing bouquet" of flowers and greens.

I give information here on prepping echeveria rosettes so that they can be used in a bouquet. How to care for roses and other cut flowers so that they stay fresh for as long as possible is readily available online; type "preparing roses for a bouquet" into a search engine.

▲ A bouquet holder and a frilly collar are among florist Robyn Foreman's behind-the-scenes items. "Cover your mechanics always," she advises.

▶ Floral material, left to right: 'Tenga Venga' rose, orange hypericum berries, prepped echeverias, eucalyptus

◀◀ In this special-occasion bouquet, pink on the edges of *Echeveria* 'Cass' leaves repeats the pink of the 'Tenga Venga' roses. Greens are eucalyptus, lemon leaves, and *Kalanchoe fedtschenkoi* stems.

MATERIALS

- 4-inch-diameter bouquet holder containing floral foam
- ruffled sheer for the base of the holder
- floral knife or clippers
- heavy-duty wire cutters
- garden clippers
- bucket of water

GREENS:

- twelve stems of lemon leaves
- four stems of leather fern
- two 4-inch pots of *Kalanchoe fedtschenkoi*, cut apart for the stems
- four sprigs of spiral eucalyptus

FOCAL ELEMENTS:

- twelve pink roses
- six 3- to 4-inch-diameter pink-and-blue eche-veria rosettes, prepped
- four 2- to 3-inch-diameter fuzzy echeveria rosettes, prepped
- four small (1- to 2-inch-diameter) blue echeve-ria rosettes, prepped

FILLER:

- eight sprigs of hypericum berries
- remaining greens
- sprays of pearls or ribbons (optional)

1. Soak the bouquet holder in water for a few minutes to hydrate the floral foam. Then set the holder in a bucket of something heavy like sand to support it while you work on the arrangement.

2. Cut and insert stems of the greens into the foam so they emerge from it like rays. Greens create a background for the bouquet, serve as its foundation, and also define its shape (oval or teardrop).

▶ Greens frame the bouquet. Next come the bouquet's dramatic elements—roses and the largest succulent rosettes.

3. Add focal elements next—roses and succulent rosettes—in threes of each, working from largest to smallest. As you do so, cut the rosettes' faux stems to the length you want, using heavy-duty wire cutters.

4. Hold the bouquet in front of a mirror. Gaps that need filling will become obvious. Avoid taking out stems and reinserting them, which can cause the foam to fall apart. If you must rearrange them, give each stem a fresh cut before reinserting.

5. Add smaller filler flowers, more greens if needed, and finish with sprays of pearls or ribbons if desired.

How to prep succulent rosettes

Prepping (creating stems for) succulent rosettes is not difficult and is enjoyable to do with friends and family members. Once they learn this simple technique, they'll go on to create their own long-lasting succulent bouquets.

Succulent rosettes might be prepped a week or more in advance without losing freshness, but the prepped rosettes need to be stored in bright light (not full sun). Unlike flowers, which should be stored in dim light or darkness, succulents will revert to green and lose their tight shape as they attempt to expose more surface area to the sun. Rootless rosettes are vulnerable to sunburn, so do not store them where their leaves may be scorched.

FOR EACH SUCCULENT ROSETTE, YOU'LL NEED:
- 9-inch length of 20-gauge wire
- 4-inch floral pick
- florist's tape
- clippers

▶ After a length of 20-gauge florist's wire is inserted horizontally through the echeveria stem and bent down, it can be coiled around a substitute stem.

▼ These *Echeveria* 'Lola' rosettes are prepped, meaning they have faux stems. Robyn likes 'Lola' because it holds its pale pinkish lavender color and does not turn green, even in low light.

▼ The wired stem is ready to be wrapped with stretchy green florist's tape.

1. Remove the succulent from its nursery pot and trim away its roots, leaving about an inch of stem. Peel away any dry leaves at the base of the rosette.

2. Swish underside of rosettes in water to clean any soil that clings to them. Place on a towel to absorb moisture. Don't prep them until dry (the tape won't adhere).

3. Push the wire horizontally through the stem below the lowest leaves. Bend the wire down so it forms a U with the stem in the middle.

4. Set the blunt end of the floral pick at the base of the rosette alongside the stem. Secure the rosette to the pick by tightly wrapping the wire around it.

5. Starting at the base of the rosette, attach the florist's tape below the rosette, then pull and stretch the tape with one hand as you twirl the wire-wrapped stem between the thumb and forefinger of your other. Don't stretch the florist's tape beforehand; it won't stick.

6. Cut or tear the tape at the bottom of the pick.

◀ The finished bouquet has something old (the tradition of using roses) and something new and blue (echeveria rosettes).

Make a corsage or boutonniere

Using floral material inspired by the main bouquet, make boutonnieres for the gentlemen and corsages (wrist or lapel) for the ladies. This simple technique also works well for hair ornaments.

MATERIALS
- satin ribbon
- pencil for curling the stem
- scissors
- floral tape
- 9-inch length of 20-gauge floral wire
- echeveria rosette
- greens (several sprigs that go with the bride's bouquet)
- florist's straight pin

Prep an echeveria rosette using wire only (no pick) and twist the wire to form a flexible stem. Make a minibouquet with the greens behind the echeveria and framing it. Wrap all the stems together with floral tape and then with the ribbon. Leave an inch of the ribbon at the top and trim to a V. Cut the bundled stems so they're 2 inches long, then coil around a pencil, creating what Robyn calls "a cute little pig's tail." Pin in place.

◀ A single *Echeveria minima* rosette was prepped without a wood pick (wire only).

Three

100 EASY-CARE SUCCULENTS

THIS ANNOTATED LIST of one hundred of my favorite easy-care succulents includes those of all sizes, including windowsill plants, ground covers, vines, shrubs, and trees. Most are plants I've grown in containers, in the ground, or both. Quite a few are plants I wish had been available or I had known about when I began gardening in earnest in the '90s. I learned about them through trial and error, and via enthusiastic recommendations from experts and friends.

In compiling this list, I rejected succulents that initially seduced me by their good looks but later proved disappointing. Silver dollar jade (*Crassula arborescens*), for example, has disc-shaped gray leaves rimmed in red and a branching structure similar to *Crassula ovata* (jade plant). A shrub succulent, silver dollar jade grows with teeth-gnashing slowness, which would be forgivable if its leaves didn't invariably look pitted—not only in my own garden but everywhere else I've seen it.

Then there's gorgeous *Echeveria nodulosa*, its leaves decorated with lines that appear to have been drawn with red felt pen. It has relatively (for a succulent) thin leaves, doubtless why they so often appear marred. And *Kalanchoe* 'Pink Butterflies', a close relative of mother of thousands (*Kalanchoe daigremontiana*), has rainbow-variegated foliage and dainty pink plantlets that frill its slender leaves in summer. But despite my pinching it back for fullness and attempting to fatten it up with rich soil and ideal light, the specimen I planted never again looked as good as when new from the nursery.

Availability is another criterion. Despite the fact that collectors disdain common succulents and breeders offer varieties that deserve to be better known, the majority listed here can be found at larger garden centers, specialty nurseries, and online sources. That said, I couldn't resist including a few uncommon up-and-comers.

If you garden in a desert climate, pay particular attention to the entries for cacti, agaves, hesperaloes, and yuccas; if you're in a northern climate, to sedums (stonecrops) and sempervivums (hens-and-chicks).

◀◀ Colorful echeverias and sedums, as well as aloes in bloom, illustrate how lovely a water-wise succulent garden can be.

Aeoniums

Aeoniums (a-OH-nee-ums), from the Canary Islands off the west coast of North Africa, like slightly more moisture than other succulents. Many are understory plants that do best in dappled sun and bright shade, but a few like full sun and grow on exposed rock cliffs in their native habitat. Those with deeper pigment (such as *Aeonium* 'Zwartkop') have greater sun tolerance. Aeoniums thrive in mild maritime climates such as coastal California, where more than a dozen varieties are readily available. Unlike many succulents, they are summer-dormant winter growers and do best where winters are rainy and summers dry. Use aeoniums to add lushness and pinwheel patterns to garden beds, terraces, and containers. New growth is from the center of the rosettes and older leaves wither and fall off, so eventually you get a denuded stem with a rosette perched on top. If you prefer a more compact plant, behead the rosettes below their lowest leaves, replant as cuttings, and discard the rest. One thing I love about succulents, and aeoniums in particular, is that no flowers are needed to put on a great show. Yet when they do bloom, the flowers are spectacular. Aeonium rosettes are monocarpic (they flower once and then die), but this can take years to happen, and seldom do all rosettes on the plant bloom at once.

▲ Mounds of bright green aeonium rosettes repeat and contrast with—in color, shape, and texture—the yellow and green foliage of dark green junipers, yellow euonymus, and *Agave desmettiana* 'Variegata'. I started the aeoniums from a single layer of cuttings three years earlier.

▼ A bridesmaid's bouquet that needs no water consists of 'Kiwi' aeoniums and yellow strawflowers.

Aeonium arboreum 'Zwartkop'
BLACK AEONIUM

MATURE SIZE Rosettes 6 to 8 inches in diameter
HARDINESS 32 degrees F

This glossy aeonium appears black at first glance but is actually a dark burgundy that glows red when backlit. Its coloration gives it better sun tolerance than that of other aeoniums, or other smooth-leaved succulents for that matter. If it is grown in less than full sun, its center will turn green and its leaves elongate.

Because of its astonishing color, nearly everyone who sees *Aeonium arboreum* 'Zwartkop' wants it. Black aeoniums are indeed captivating, but keep in mind they tend to disappear, visually, in garden beds and bouquetlike arrangements because they read as a dark spot or gap. Give 'Zwartkop' a light backdrop, such as the sky or a wall, or juxtapose it with plants with yellow or silvery foliage.

Aeonium canariense
CANARY ISLAND AEONIUM

▲ Canary Island aeoniums (*Aeonium canariense*) appear to spill from a basin and float downstream.

MATURE SIZE Rosettes 6 to 12 inches in diameter, depending on variety
HARDINESS 32 degrees F

Aeonium canariense and its hybrids form compact shrubs of overlapping rosettes on branching stems. The velvety leaves, which are fresh green when grown in semishade, become red-edged in full sun.

Aeonium 'Kiwi' (*Aeonium decorum* 'Kiwi')
'KIWI' AEONIUM

MATURE SIZE Rosettes to 3 inches in diameter; shrubs to 15 inches tall and wide
HARDINESS 32 degrees F

Each pointed-leaved, variegated rosette grows to the diameter of a teacup. Leaves combine green and yellow or cream, and (with adequate sun exposure) rose red along leaf margins. *Aeonium* 'Kiwi' rosettes are great for adding color and the look of flowers to topiaries, vertical gardens, living pictures, and moss-and-glue arrangements. They also make excellent container and window box plants.

Aeonium 'Sunburst'
'SUNBURST' AEONIUM

MATURE SIZE Rosettes 6 to 8 inches in diameter
HARDINESS 32 degrees F

Aeonium 'Sunburst', with its yellow- or cream-and-green striped leaves often but not always tipped in pink, is among the loveliest of succulents. It resembles a large daisy with rubbery petals, and its light color makes it a garden standout. Grow in a red or pink container to emphasize the rosy tips. Combine it with other variegated succulents for visually appealing color repetitions, and use it to brighten areas of the garden in dappled shade. Leaves are easily marred, so handle gently.

Agaves

Agaves (ah-GAV-ehs) are easy-care, New World succulents that prefer a full-sun location. Indoors and in shade, agaves will lean in the direction of greatest light. Most agaves are stemless and have tapered, pointed leaves. Some resemble artichokes, others a bouquet of swords. Spikes at leaf tips and along leaf margins make these somewhat dangerous plants, especially along walkways; yet from a design standpoint, their crisp forms are unmatched and lend a sculptural element to any garden. When grooming agaves, snip a quarter inch from the tips to protect yourself and others from impalement. Avoid getting agave sap on your skin; it may cause an allergic reaction. Remove any dirt or debris that falls into an agave's crown, lest it harbor moisture and pests. Nearly all agaves are hardy to several degrees below freezing, and many go a lot lower.

Agaves propagate subtly, beneath a blanket of soil, and also bloom exuberantly, for all the world to see. Shallow rhizomes may produce pups; watch for them, and dig them out if you don't want the plants to spread. Know the size at maturity of any agave you plant. Some species become immense. Since agaves die after flowering, plan accordingly; don't position one where it will be difficult to remove five or ten years hence. Container-grown agaves generally take much longer to bloom than those in the ground. Large agaves make good firebreak plants and security fences.

▶ Sculptural, blue-gray century plant (*Agave americana*) thrives in poor soil, gets by on rainfall, and is hardy from below freezing to above 100 degrees. It is best kept confined in and dwarfed by a sturdy pot rather than planted in a residential garden, where it may offset and grow up to 6 feet tall and wide.

Agave americana 'Mediopicta Alba'
TUXEDO AGAVE

Agave attenuata
FOX TAIL AGAVE

MATURE SIZE 3 feet in diameter
HARDINESS 32 degrees F

Agave attenuata is gentle compared to other agaves, with flexible leaves that lack teeth or terminal spines—doubtless the reason it's widely grown throughout southern California. What stops it from traipsing across the world like more thuglike *Agave americana* is its sensitivity to temperature extremes. Fox tail agaves don't do well in desert heat, and with the slightest breath of frost, their leaf tips collapse like wet Kleenex.

Unlike other agaves, which typically are stemless rosettes, fox tail agaves form trunks and thus are easy to propagate by cuttings. Slice through the trunk 6 to 8 inches below the lowest leaves, dig a hole slightly larger than the diameter of the trunk and 6 inches deep, and insert the cutting. Presto, instant plant. Keep the soil moist to encourage root formation.

The common name is derived from the agave's unbranched flower stalks, which appear fuzzy when massed with flowers. But a more descriptive name, based on the stalks' distinctively curved shape, might be question-mark agave. When several bloom in a garden at once, the sight of such tall, fuzzy arches—all nodding sunward—is otherworldly.

MATURE SIZE 3 feet in diameter
HARDINESS 15 degrees F

When strategically positioned, this cream-and-gray-striped agave will offer the same dynamic, sculptural presence as its immense cousins *Agave americana* (century plant) and *Agave americana* 'Marginata' (striped century plant), which grow effortlessly throughout the Southwest and are found worldwide. Tuxedo agaves also offset but not as prolifically, so when it happens, it's usually a blessed event.

▶ Once pricey and hard to come by, variegates of *Agave attenuata* are becoming more widely available; this one is 'Kara's Stripes'. Protect from direct, hot sun and frost.

Agave 'Blue Flame'
'BLUE FLAME' AGAVE

MATURE SIZE 4 feet in diameter
HARDINESS 25 degrees F

Born of a tryst between widely grown but frost-tender *Agave attenuata* and hardier *Agave shawii*, 'Blue Flame' combines the best of both: beautiful form, great color, and enhanced cold tolerance. Blue-green leaves reminiscent of a gas burner's flames are flexible, with finely serrated edges; inward-curving tips are long and needle-like. Combine this graceful agave with more upright and smaller 'Blue Glow' agave (*Agave* 'Blue Glow'), which has similar watercolor-like striations and contrasting red-edged leaves.

Agave bracteosa
GREEN SPIDER AGAVE

MATURE SIZE 18 inches in diameter
HARDINESS 10 degrees F

Unlike most agaves, this native of northeastern Mexico is unarmed. *Agave bracteosa* has smooth, slender leaves that resemble flat, tapered green ribbons. Upright new leaves in the rosette's center form a distinctive star. The plant's undulating, squidlike leaves make it useful for undersea-themed succulent gardens. It pups freely, which is a bonus if you want more. 'Monterrey Frost', a seldom-seen, slow-growing, but gorgeous variegate, has white-margined leaves.

Agave 'Cream Spike'
'CREAM SPIKE' AGAVE

MATURE SIZE 6 inches in diameter
HARDINESS 15 degrees F

This diminutive variegated agave shows to advantage in a container that repeats the brown-black of its terminal spines. Plant it tilted slightly (the better to be seen) in a bonsai dish. Bolster it with rocks, leaving spaces for pups to protrude. Over time, these offspring will spontaneously complete the composition.

Agave lophantha 'Quadricolor'
'QUADRICOLOR' AGAVE

MATURE SIZE 15 inches in diameter
HARDINESS 20 degrees F

The yellow-edged leaves of this exquisite agave are dark green in the center with a pale green midstripe. Leaf margins will redden when the plant is grown in bright sun, giving it a fourth color. 'Quadricolor' agaves look amazing when planted in multiples. The species, *Agave lophantha*, is larger and solid green, and is a desert rat that can tolerate a hundred-degree temperature range. Be careful when handling—those stiff, serrated leaves are sharp.

Agave parryi and varieties
PARRY'S AGAVE, ARTICHOKE AGAVE

▲ *Agave parryi* var. *truncata*

MATURE SIZE 2 to 3 feet in diameter
HARDINESS varies

Varieties of *Agave parryi* are artichoke-like and a pleasing dove gray that may be whiter, greenish, or more blue, depending on the variety. Leaves range from rounded to slender ovals; most plants form offsets. The native habitat of these popular landscape plants ranges from northern Arizona to western Texas. All are fairly cold tolerant (to 10 degrees F or less).

Agave potatorum 'Kissho Kan' (*Agave* 'Kichi-Jokan')
BUTTERFLY AGAVE

▲ *Agave potatorum* 'Kissho Kan' with *Beaucarnea recurvata* on the left and *Cleistocactus strausii*, in bloom, on the right

MATURE SIZE 18 inches in diameter
HARDINESS 30 degrees F

This silvery blue agave has many short leaves packed into a dense, symmetrical rosette, giving it more of a "rose" look than agaves with longer, narrower leaves. It's magnificent in pots. If you're growing it in the garden, allow plenty of room for pups. A variegated dwarf form is worth looking for and is becoming more widely available.

Agave shawii
SHAW'S AGAVE

MATURE SIZE 2½ feet in diameter
HARDINESS 25 degrees F

The first time I saw a colony of *Agave shawii*, in Baja California, I was intrigued by the plants' marginal teeth. With the sun shining directly at them, they appeared gray, but with the sun behind them, they exhibited hues of coral, yellow, pink, and rose red. Sometimes the green inner leaves of Shaw's agave are beautifully framed by older chartreuse ones with a red-orange blush. Leaves also may have striations that resemble brushstrokes. Grow *Agave shawii* in pots or in a part of the garden where its tendency to pup won't matter. And be sure to position it where the early morning or late afternoon sun will backlight the margins.

Agave utahensis
UTAH AGAVE

MATURE SIZE 8 inches in diameter
HARDINESS –10 degrees F

Agave utahensis has narrow, serrated leaves and forms dense clusters of smallish rosettes. It grows at elevations of 3,000 to 5,000 feet in very dry surroundings, with blazing summers and winters that drop well below freezing. Although one of the most cold-tolerant agaves, Utah agave has to be kept dry during its winter dormancy lest it rot. Variety 'Eborispina' has long, twisting, white terminal spines.

Agave victoriae-reginae
QUEEN VICTORIA AGAVE

MATURE SIZE 12 inches in diameter
HARDINESS 10 degrees F

British horticulturist Thomas Moore named this lovely Mexican agave for England's Queen Victoria. It is indeed a regal succulent, with dark green leaves outlined with white lines and black tips. Because Queen Victoria agave is nearly spherical, it shows to advantage framed by a pot's round rim. It also is effective arranged in multiples, either in the garden or in containers. Tuck rosettes into the pockets of a strawberry jar or into a rock garden's crevices. Cultivars with white or gold stripes can be seen at Cactus and Succulent Society shows and occasionally at specialty nurseries.

Agave expert Greg Starr, who notes that each leaf of Queen Victoria agave has been "lovingly hand-painted by the agave gods with decorative white bud prints," describes this as one of the slowest growing *Agave* species, taking twenty to twenty-five years to reach flowering size. When one bloomed in my neighborhood I took photos, but the flower spike was so tall (15 feet) and slender, I had to shoot from across the street. Sadly, due to a backdrop of foliage, I have a very poor record of such a momentous event.

Alluaudia procera
MADAGASCAN OCOTILLO

MATURE SIZE 15 to 25 feet tall by 4 to 6 feet wide
HARDINESS 20 to 35 degrees F

No other succulent looks quite like alluaudia (ah-loo-AH-dee-ah), but the plant itself—with its tall, skinny trunks—is suggestive of ocotillo (*Fouquieria splendens*), a southwestern desert native tipped with red flowers. As the common name implies, *Alluaudia procera* is from Madagascar. Its thorny gray trunks are lined with oval, bright green leaves that it may lose in winter, making it look prickly and bleached. It takes years for alluaudia to bloom, and when it does, sprays of dainty flowers give the plant airy topknots. Designers love its verticality.

Aloes

Aloes (AH-lohs) produce the most spectacular blooms of any plant, succulent or otherwise. Tubular flowers in shades of orange, red, or yellow, and occasionally cream or bicolor, may be as densely packed as corn kernels on stems 2 feet tall. Even the daintiest aloe flowers, arrayed on the tips of airy, branching stems no thicker than dry spaghetti, attract hummingbirds. Depending on the weather, the show may last several weeks or more.

Aloes are native to southern Africa, the Arabian Peninsula, and Madagascar. They range from a few inches high to trees, and their thick, lancelike leaves are smooth, bumpy, or prickled, usually with toothed margins. Leaves, which are crescent shaped in cross section, funnel water downward to the crown of the plant. In general, aloes like slightly wetter conditions than agaves. Frost may burn the tips of aloe leaves, causing them to shrivel, and most aloes cannot handle a hard freeze (several hours below 25 degrees F). Leaves of many aloes redden when the plant is stressed by cold, drought, or more sun or less rich soil that it really wants. Small aloes look great en masse, as container plants, and in rock or boulder gardens.

Because their roots do not swell significantly over time and they form a network that extends only a few inches below the soil surface, aloes can be planted along the foundations of structures and near swimming pools. Aloes also produce minimal leaf litter and need no maintenance other than deadheading spent flower stalks. Once a stalk has dried, I wiggle it loose and use its blunt, spoon-shaped stem end to flick debris from leaf axils.

At first glance, aloes and agaves may look alike, but the differences are significant. Aloes have gel-filled, tapered leaves, with edges (often serrated) that are an extension of the skin of the leaf; agaves have margins and terminal spines of a tougher tissue (think fingernail or horn as opposed to skin). Agaves are from the southwestern United States and Mexico; aloes, from the Old World. And unlike most agaves, which die after blooming, aloes flower annually.

Best succulents for encouraging a child's interest in gardening

Children love plants with personality, especially those that expand their awareness of what a plant can be. Whenever you see something new that captivates you—perhaps makes you want to touch it—you're experiencing how children initially respond to many succulents that you've come to take for granted.

Succulents that invariably engender child-like wonder are listed here. They stand up to handling, survive neglect, are rewarding to nurture, and become even more interesting over time. Each has one or more kid-friendly characteristics; it's mottled, toothed, ribbed, furry, webbed, necklace- or beadlike, goofy, or extraterrestrial-looking. You'll find their sun/shade requirements and other notable attributes in the main list.

Aloe, dwarf cultivars
Aloe hemmingii (mosaic aloe)
Beaucarnea recurvata (bottle palm)
Ceropegia woodii (rosary vine, string of hearts)
Cotyledon tomentosa (kitten paws, bear paws)
Crassula species, stacked (stacked crassulas)
Crassula ovata 'Hobbit' and 'Gollum' (jades)
Echeveria 'Doris Taylor' and 'Frosty' (fuzzy echeverias)
Haworthia attenuata (zebra plant)
Haworthia limifolia (fairy washboard)
Kalanchoe beharensis 'Fang' (felt bush, velvet leaf)
Kalanchoe daigremontiana (mother of thousands)
Kalanchoe tomentosa (panda plant)
Sedum rubrotinctum 'Pork and Beans' ('Pork and Beans' stonecrop)
Sempervivum arachnoideum (cobweb houseleek)
Senecio radicans 'Fish Hooks' ('Fish Hooks' senecio)

Aloe, dwarf cultivars
DWARF ALOES

▲ *Aloe 'Blizzard'*

MATURE SIZE 2 to 4 inches high by 3 to 5 inches wide
HARDINESS 30 degrees F

Aloe cultivars exist that are intended solely as container plants. Such diminutive succulents seldom grow larger than softballs, and many are variegated and textured with raised dots and dashes. What appear to be coral-colored splinters encrust the leaves of popular 'Pink Blush' aloe. Lesser-known 'Blizzard' is dark green banded with snowy white; it pups so freely, a 4-inch nursery pot may contain a dozen. Other dwarf aloe hybrids include 'Diego', 'Fang', 'Lizard Lips', and 'Doran Black', to name a few.

Aloe arborescens
TORCH ALOE

MATURE SIZE Mounding clusters to 6 or more feet in diameter
HARDINESS 22 degrees F

Among the most common landscape succulents in southern California, torch aloes eventually form multitrunked mounds. The plants thrive in beach gardens and tolerate salt spray, and also do well in hot, dry inland areas. Leaves are serrated but not sharp; conical flowers atop slender stalks are the bright orange of traffic cones. A variegated variety is striped with pale green and cream, and there are also torch aloes with yellow flowers (not nearly as common as orange).

Aloe 'Blue Elf'
'BLUE ELF' ALOE

▲ 'Blue Elf' aloes add color to a cycad garden.

MATURE SIZE 18 inches high, spreading to 2 feet wide
HARDINESS 20 degrees F

This slender-leaved aloe has graceful, upright blue-gray foliage. When in bloom, massed plants suggest drifts of orange-red confetti. After their February to April flowering, the plants bloom sporadically—a bonus atypical of aloes. To create garden beds with pleasing repetitions of foliage color and contrasting shapes and textures, combine 'Blue Elf' aloes with blue-and-cream-striped tuxedo agaves (*Agave americana* 'Mediopicta Alba'). Surround them with hens-and-chicks echeverias and a succulent ground cover such as 'Angelina' stonecrop.

Aloe brevifolia
SHORT-LEAF ALOE

MATURE SIZE Rosettes to 4 inches wide; mounding clusters to 2 feet or more in diameter
HARDINESS 25 degrees F

Short-leaf aloes form rosettes that offset freely and become a tight colony. Leaves are pale blue-green in bright shade, rosy pink-and-yellow in full sun. *Aloe brevifolia* is often confused with *Aloe nobilis*, but the latter is a green that reddens to orange, and rosettes are slightly larger. To harvest offsets from a clumping aloe, cut small ones loose from the edge of the cluster at ground level, rather than from the center, which might damage tightly packed leaves and create a gap that compromises the mound's symmetry.

Aloe dorotheae
SUNSET ALOE

MATURE SIZE 12 inches high by 8 inches wide
HARDINESS 28 degrees F

Leaves of this aloe, named after "a Miss Dorthy [sic] Westhead of London" according to an 1890 description, turn such a glossy bright red when the plant is grown in full sun, it makes you wonder if its namesake was prone to blushing. Foliage is flecked with white, and rickrack edges are white-tipped, too, causing the plant to look even more starfishlike than most small aloes. Use this clustering Tanzanian native in undersea-themed succulent gardens and in pots that are a comparably saturated and contrasting color, such as cobalt or sky blue.

Aloe ferox
CAPE ALOE

MATURE SIZE 6+ feet tall
HARDINESS 20 degrees F

From South Africa's former Cape Province, these aloes form one large rosette and are trunk forming over time. Blue-gray leaves are often flushed with rose and can be smooth or prickled. In early spring, Cape aloes send up tall, columnar flower spikes. Don't trim off dry downward-curling leaves; they protect the trunk from excessive sun, heat, and cold.

Aloe hemmingii
MOSAIC ALOE

MATURE size 6 inches in diameter
HARDINESS 32 degrees F

Leaves of mosaic aloes remind me of a sun-dappled stream. Against a background of glossy green (or reddish brown, if the plant gets lots of sun), white markings could be white dots flowing so rapidly they've stretched into dashes. And if that isn't lovely enough, leaf margins are tricked out in red. Mosaic aloes show to advantage in pots; for a wow presentation, topdress with crushed brick. The plant is often mislabeled as *Aloe harlana*, which looks similar but is larger and uncommon.

Aloe 'Hercules'
'HERCULES' ALOE

Aloe humilis
SPIDER ALOE

MATURE SIZE 20+ feet tall
HARDINESS 23 degrees F

MATURE SIZE 8 inches high
HARDINESS 20 degrees F

A vigorous tree aloe with a thick trunk, 'Hercules' is topped with explosions of fleshy green leaves. The aptly named succulent exhibits hybrid vigor, meaning it possesses qualities superior to those of either horticultural parent. These are finicky *Aloe dichotoma*, which is intolerant of summer watering, and *Aloe bainesii*, which is prone to black sooty leaf spots in all but arid climates. 'Hercules' also handles lower temperatures. Use it to lend height, texture, and a dynamic silhouette to a dry garden.

The blue-green foliage of this dainty aloe sparkles with irregularly spaced, nubby prickles. The slender upright leaves are slightly inward curving, creating a compact rosette that over time offsets to form a cluster. Use as a textural accent in containers, to repeat the blue of other succulents, and to contrast with smooth-leaved companions. Keep dry in winter.

Aloe nobilis
GOLD TOOTH ALOE

MATURE SIZE 6+ inches in diameter
HARDINESS 20 degrees F

When grown in dappled shade and rich soil, gold tooth aloes are green with yellow-toothed margins—attractive, but not as amazingly orange as when sunbaked. A variegated version also exists. I've seen this common, clump-forming succulent serve as a no-mow lawn replacement in an infrequently watered "hell strip" between sidewalk and street. That's not a bad idea, providing there's a no-aloe area wide enough for passengers to enter or exit a parked car.

Aloe plicatilis
FAN ALOE

MATURE SIZE 5 feet tall
HARDINESS 23 degrees F

Thanks to leaves shaped like tongue depressors arranged in stacked pairs that form fans, this aloe looks like no other. These winter growers become minitrees that often have leaf tips the same orange as the flowers. Rather than clinging to the stems, leaves fall away, revealing a smooth gray trunk and branches. Combine with other summer-dormant succulents, such as aeoniums and senecios, all of which should be kept on the dry side in summer. Give supplemental irrigation in winter if rainfall is sparse.

Aloe polyphylla
SPIRAL ALOE

MATURE SIZE 18 inches in diameter
HARDINESS 10 degrees F

Few plants are as seductively lovely as spiral aloes. Wedge-shaped leaves form a whorl that suggests an elaborate bow. Native to 8,000-foot elevations in Lesotho, South Africa, spiral aloes are accustomed to being buried in snow, and their cells contain a natural antifreeze. The plants may not flower until a foot or more in diameter, and even then may not bloom every year. The Holy Grail of succulent collectors is to have clockwise and counterclockwise spiral aloes side by side. The plants dislike southern California's hot summers but are fairly easy to grow in northern California, especially the Bay Area, providing drainage is superb.

Aloe speciosa
TILT-HEAD ALOE

MATURE SIZE 8+ feet tall
HARDINESS 25 degrees F

Whenever I assert that succulents have the most beautiful flowers in the plant kingdom, this tree-like aloe comes to mind. Arising from its large, single crown are multiple conical flower spikes. Cream-colored buds around the bottom swirl upward into less-mature rose pink ones, and all sport thin green lines. As buds open, dark red stamens emerge, forming a fringe. In order to bloom, these aloes need to be planted in the garden (not in a pot), in a sunny, frost-free area. The common name, tilt-head aloe, refers to the tendency of the crown to lean toward greatest sun exposure.

Aloe striata
CORAL ALOE

MATURE SIZE 18 inches high and wide
HARDINESS 22 degrees F

This midsize aloe with branching flower stalks has subtle pinstriped leaves and translucent orange margins. The true species is ribbon-edged and doesn't offset. More common is a subspecies with toothed margins that does pup. I like the sleek look of the former, but I've found the latter less expensive, easier to come by, and more adaptable to the garden. Coral aloes are more frost hardy than most and don't get overly large, making them wonderful garden, container, and landscape plants.

Aloe vanbalenii
VAN BALEN'S ALOE ▶

MATURE SIZE Mounds 1 to 2 feet high and 3 to 4 feet in diameter
HARDINESS 25 degrees F

Van Balen's aloe makes a great garden focal point against a solid backdrop. This colony-forming, octopus-like aloe's leaves curl, twist, and overlap. When the plant grows in rich soil with regular water and sun protection, leaves are green. In full, hot sun with nutrient-poor soil and minimal water, leaves turn orange. It's lovely contrasted with columnar blue cacti, golden barrels, and blue senecio. Slender, conical flowers on unbranched spikes are yellow to yellow-orange.

Aloe variegata
PARTRIDGE BREAST ALOE, TIGER ALOE ◄

MATURE SIZE 1 foot tall
HARDINESS 20 degrees F

This sculptural, elegant little aloe has a distinguished history as a houseplant, having grown on European windowsills since its discovery, in 1685, by Dutch plant hunters on expedition to South Africa. Its crisply geometric shape, thick leaves that appear stacked, and coral-colored flowers on thick stalks make it lovely in pots, solo or in combination with other succulents. The common name, partridge breast aloe, comes from speckled bands on the leaves, which also have narrow white margins. When in doubt, err on the dry side; this aloe's weakness is its sensitivity to overwatering. Turns reddish brown when environmentally stressed.

▶ Rat-tail cactus (*Aporocactus flagelliformis*) mimics cascading water in a dry fountain.

Aporocactus flagelliformis (*Disocactus flagelliformis*)
RAT-TAIL CACTUS

MATURE SIZE To several feet in length
HARDINESS 35 degrees F

Aporocactus (ah-POR-oh-kak-tus) *flagelliformis*, a tropical cactus native to Latin America, is epiphytic (grows in trees). Bright pink flowers that appear in summer attract hummingbirds. It can be cultivated indoors if given bright light all day, and it makes a wonderful textural addition to hanging baskets. Keep soil moist and give ample water in summer. Without good air circulation, rat-tail cactus is susceptible to scale and mealybug infestations.

Astrophytum species
STAR CACTUS

MATURE SIZE 6 to 12 inches in diameter
HARDINESS 20 degrees F

Astrophytums (as-tro-FY-tums) are plump, spherical, segmented cacti from Mexico that are spineless or nearly so. They make wonderful pot plants and will grow contentedly indoors if given bright light for much of the day. The fewer the sections that a bishop's hat cactus (*Astrophytum myriostigma*) has—four or six being ideal—the more desirable it is to collectors, who are also careful not to disturb the plant's fragile, chalky scales. When not in bloom, sand dollar cactus (*Astrophytum asterias*) looks a lot like *Euphorbia obesa*, but the two are native to different continents. Sand dollar cactus has been in cultivation since the 1840s, and wonderful varieties exist. 'Super Kabuto', for example, is beautifully patterned with white dots. As with most cacti, flowers are satiny and showy.

Beaucarnea recurvata
BOTTLE PALM ▶

MATURE SIZE 10 to 12 feet tall (with age)
HARDINESS 25 degrees F

Unlike other tree succulents, beaucarneas (boh-CAR-nee-ahs) make good houseplants. Despite the name and resemblance, bottle palms aren't palms. They also don't have succulent leaves; the classification is due to their bulbous, water-storing trunks. Add a bottle palm to your garden as a focal point if your climate is relatively frost-free, or let one slowly swell, like an overfed rabbit, to fill a container. Either way, such mop-headed plants serve as easy-care, goofy-looking conversation starters and garden focal points. *Beaucarnea recurvata* has curved leaves; those of similar *Beaucarnea stricta* are straight.

◀ A collection of astrophytums, including bishop's hat and sand dollar varieties

Ceropegia woodii
ROSARY VINE, STRING OF HEARTS

MATURE SIZE Several feet in length
HARDINESS 32 degrees F

This succulent vine looks like a cross between ivy and a beaded curtain. Dime-sized heart-shaped leaves (which may be variegated) are intriguing but not as strange as the flowers, which look like inch-long purple flamingos. Grow ceropegia (ser-oh-PEE-gee-ah) in bright shade or indoors, in a hanging basket or in a pot atop a shelf.

Although rosary vine can be propagated by stem cuttings and seeds, the easiest way is to let one of the nubby, beadlike tubercles (spiky little balls) along the stem take root. Set a strand atop a pot of soil beneath the plant so tubercles will continue to be fed while forming roots—although the larger they are to begin with, the less they'll need this. Once the little plants are established, they can be detached from the mother vine.

Cleistocactus strausii
SILVER TORCH CACTUS ▶

MATURE SIZE 4 to 8 feet tall
HARDINESS −10 degrees F (if dry)

Succulents in the genus *Cleistocactus* (cly-IS-toh-kak-tus) lend height and drama to gardens and containers. Blooms, which protrude horizontally, look like fuzzy magenta cigarettes. Silver torch cacti are reasonably fast growing and trouble free, providing they are not overwatered. Enhance drainage by planting them atop mounded soil liberally amended with pumice. When sunlit, the white spines of silver torches shimmer. I've grown a grouping of six, bolstered by rocks in a shallow container, on an east-facing deck that gets so hot in summer, few plants other than cacti can handle it. Regardless of the season, every morning I enjoy looking at that dish garden aglow.

Cotyledon orbiculata
PIG'S EAR

MATURE SIZE 2 feet tall and wide
HARDINESS 30 degrees F

Plants in the genus *Cotyledon* (koh-teh-LEE-don) often are confused with jades (*Crassula*), but the flowers are very different. Jades have clusters of small star-shaped flowers, usually in midwinter; cotyledons send up panicles of orange, bell-shaped blooms in early summer. These serve as a counterpoint to upright foliage that may be cylindrical or pancakelike and edged with a thin line of red. Leaf colors include green, blue, powdery mauve, and gray. Blooms attract ants that colonize them with aphids; spray or dab the pests with diluted isopropyl alcohol lest the flower show be spoiled.

Cotyledon tomentosa
KITTEN PAWS, BEAR PAWS

MATURE SIZE 6 inches high
HARDINESS 30 degrees F

Plump green leaves that vary from grape- to thumb-size are pawlike and fuzzy, and tipped with dark red points. *Cotyledon tomentosa* serves as a good filler for container arrangements. Also look for a less common, variegated (cream-and-green striped) variety.

Crassulas

The numerous species and cultivars of *Crassula* (KRAS-u-lah) can be loosely categorized as jade-like or stacked. The former have thick stems and grow into branching shrubs that can be pruned into small trees and used for bonsai. Flowers appear midwinter through spring, borne in clusters that may be massed so profusely the plant appears snow-covered. Jades are tough, resilient, unfussy succulents with remarkable water storage capabilities and survival skills. They also may prune themselves—limbs soften, shrivel, and fall off, resulting in a balanced shrub and fallen branches that root readily.

Stacked crassulas have leaves that appear threaded along ever-lengthening, wiry, pendant stems that turn upward as they seek light. Leaves might be long or short; square, triangular, or oval; and loosely or tightly packed. In some varieties older leaves frame newer and smaller ones, resulting in intriguing pyramids of foliage. The largest stacked crassulas have 6-inch-long leaves; the smallest, 1/16 of an inch. Flower clusters emerge from stem tips. For hanging baskets in windy areas or likely to be brushed by passersby, stacked crassulas are a better choice than graptopetalums or senecios because crassula leaves do not detach as easily.

▼ *Crassula* 'Calico Kitten' (on the left, red, in bloom) and *Crassula capitella* 'Campfire' (center, with red and green leaves)

Crassula, stacked varieties
STACKED CRASSULAS

▲ Necklace vine (*Crassula perforata*)

MATURE SIZE Mounds 4 to 8 inches high, spreading to 18 inches or more
HARDINESS 25 to 32 degrees F, depending on variety

Crassulas with pendant stems and leaves that appear stacked atop each other are useful cascaders for tall containers, hanging baskets, and pedestal pots. *Crassula corymbulosa* 'Red Pagoda', with crimson-tipped chartreuse leaves, is among the most tightly packed and angular. Leaves of necklace vine (*Crassula perforata*) form opposing pairs that can be rotated around the stem like beads. Rounded leaves of *Crassula rupestris* 'Baby's Necklace' resemble fat little buttons. *Crassula* 'Calico Kitten' is variegated cream, green, and a pink that brightens to rose in full sun. *Crassula capitella* 'Campfire' turns scorching red-orange when environmentally stressed. Its flowers elongate the stems, compromising their propeller-like architecture; prune them back by half after blooming.

▲ *Crassula corymbulosa* 'Red Pagoda' with sunset jade

Crassula ovata and its cultivars
CRASSULAS, JADE PLANTS

MATURE SIZE 2 to 4+ feet tall
HARDINESS 32 degrees F

One of the most widely grown succulents, jade plant has oval, deep green leaves margined with red, and white flowers. Cultivars of jade, though less common, are as easy to grow and to start from cuttings. *Crassula ovata* 'Pink Beauty' is a pink-flowered variety. *Crassula ovata* 'Baby Jade' has smaller leaves and a more compact form than the species. *Crassula ovata* 'Gollum' has tubular leaves; *Crassula ovata* 'Hobbit', spoon-shaped. Those of sunset jade (*Crassula ovata* 'Hummel's Sunset') are bright yellow, and those of tricolor jade (*Crassula ovata* 'Tricolor') are cream-streaked and pink-edged. Colorful jades revert to green if not grown in full sun.

▲ *Crassula ovata* 'Pink Beauty'

◀ Baby jade plant (*Crassula ovata* 'Baby Jade')

Cremnosedum 'Little Gem'
'LITTLE GEM' STONECROP

MATURE SIZE Rosettes to 1 inch in diameter, trailing to 6 inches
HARDINESS low 20s F

A tiny-leaved, mounding succulent in the genus *Cremnosedum* (krem-no-SEE-dum), 'Little Gem' forms rosettes that suggest berries or garnets. Olive green leaves redden in full sun, and clusters of tiny yellow flowers (which resemble those of sedum) appear in spring. 'Little Gem' stonecrop makes a good filler for container gardens, is charming tucked into the openings of strawberry jars, and is sure to produce a delighted gasp from any hostess who receives a pot of it.

Dasylirion species
DASYLIRIONS ▶

MATURE SIZE 4 or more feet in diameter, depending on species
HARDINESS 15 degrees F

Like *Agave geminiflora* and *Yucca rostrata*, dasylirions (das-uh-LIH-ree-uhns), from the desert Southwest and Mexico, form large, spherical pincushions. Few plants are so visually dynamic; dasylirions appear to explode out of the ground. Providing they get adequate sun and heat, these tough plants do equally well in containers or in the garden. So stiff and slender are the leaves of dasylirions, you may wonder why they're succulents; it's because their trunks store moisture. *Dasylirion longissimum* (Mexican grass tree) is a fountainlike spray of green leaves; *Dasylirion wheeleri*, with a similar silhouette, has silvery, serrated foliage. Over time, dasylirions form trunks and produce tall, slender bloom spikes that resemble Q-tips. The plants are highly drought tolerant but appreciate regular water, providing their roots don't stay sodden. Leaves aren't sharp, but even so, plant well away from stairs and walkways.

◀ Desert spoon (*Dasylirion wheeleri*)

▼ Mexican grass tree (*Dasylirion longissimum*) underplanted with *Sedum rubrotinctum* 'Pork and Beans'

Dracaena draco
DRAGON TREE

MATURE SIZE 15+ feet tall (30 feet tall with great age)
HARDINESS 25 degrees F

Dracaena draco (drah-SEE-nah dray-co) is a marvelously bizarre tree with bulbous branches tipped with clusters of long, narrow leaves. It is native to the Canary Islands, Tenerife, and the Azores; is the logo of the San Diego Botanic Garden; and is cultivated widely throughout southern California. The name comes from a reddish resin ("dragon's blood") that oozes from horizontal growth rings along the trunk. Dragon trees are not difficult to grow, but they do take a long time to mature. Bloom sprays are large and resemble those of date palms. The trees tolerate heat, wind, and salt spray. Water infrequently and deeply, and avoid keeping the root zone wet.

Dudleya pulverulenta
CHALK LIVEFOREVER

MATURE SIZE 18 inches in diameter
HARDINESS 15 degrees F

Dudleya pulverulenta gets its silvery color from a coating of fine white powder. Rosettes send up long, arching flower spikes in late spring. Native to the California coast and northern Baja California, it likes winter and spring rainfall but doesn't do well if watered in summer and autumn. In habitat, the plants grow on near-vertical cliff sides and embankments, and therefore require superb drainage. Give full sun along the coast, partial sun inland.

In summer, rosette dudleyas close up to protect their cores from sunburn and desiccation. Don't water them even if they appear crisp and miserable; they're dormant and unused to summer rainfall. However, they do appreciate an occasional misting suggestive of coastal fog.

▼ *Dudleya pulverulenta* with smaller, slender-leaved *Dudleya hassei*

Echeverias

Echeverias (ech-uh-VEH-ree-ahs, EK-uh-veh-ree-ahs) are native to Texas, Mexico, and Central and South America. Many echeverias look like plump-petaled roses in shades of pink, rose, lavender, blue, and green, and combinations thereof. They may have a metallic sheen, powdery white coating, knobby protrusions, or translucent fuzz. A few have a pointy silhouette reminiscent of agaves. Exotic cultivars with ruffled leaves suggest fluted piecrusts or cabbage roses. Echeverias produce lanternlike flowers on upright, arching stems from late spring through midsummer.

When wired onto twiglike stems and secured with stretchy green florist's tape, echeverias provide the look of roses without the water. Use small echeveria rosettes in boutonnieres and corsages, and glue them onto hair ornaments. Diminutive (smaller than 3 inches in diameter) echeverias good for living pictures and other projects include pale gray-blue *Echeveria elegans*, red-edged green *Echeveria derenbergii*, and light blue, round-leaved *Echeveria minima*.

▼ A bridal bouquet combines cream-colored roses with blue-green echeverias, green aeoniums, and a cream-and-green striped jade.

Echeveria, fuzzy
FUZZY ECHEVERIA, PLUSH PLANT

▲ Woolly rose (*Echeveria* 'Doris Taylor')

MATURE SIZE 3 to 5 inches in diameter, depending on variety
HARDINESS 20 degrees F

Fine translucent hairs that sugar the leaves of fuzzy echeverias glow silver when sunlit. 'Ruby' echeveria branches to form a small shrub, and its multiple rosettes, with their thumbnail-size leaves, are velveteen. More compact, with a hens-and-chicks growth habit, is 'Doris Taylor', a cultivar that, like a puppy, is impossible not to pet. Others, such as 'Frosty', are so white they appear to be covered with ice crystals. Fuzzy echeverias are enchanting when dotted with dew, especially if sunlit.

Echeveria, ruffled hybrids
RUFFLED ECHEVERIA

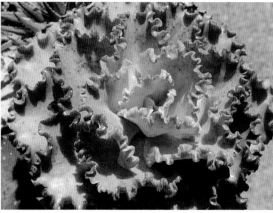

MATURE SIZE 5 to 12 inches wide
HARDINESS 30 degrees F

To see a ruffled echeveria is to want one, and nurseries and plant breeders are trying hard to oblige. Too easily marred in the open garden, they're best grown in pots. To keep frilly echeverias pristine, place in a protected location in partial shade. Aim to provide enough light so the rosettes don't flatten or stretch, and leaves retain their colors—but not so much light that they sunburn. The bright diffused light of a greenhouse is ideal, but if that's not an option, give ruffled echeverias several hours of morning sun and rotate their pots 180 degrees once a week. Or grow them in dappled shade.

▲ Depending on the time of year and how much sun they receive, the size and coloration of fancy *Echeveria* cultivars can vary. Even experts don't attempt to identify them from photos. This one might be 'Firelight', 'Misty Cloud', 'Harry Butterfield', or 'Bittersweet'—or none of them.

▶▶ **ABOVE** A ruffled *Echeveria* cultivar, possibly 'Blue Curls'

▶▶ **BELOW** *Echeveria* 'Neon Breakers' was hybridized by Renee O'Connell of Altman Plants, in Vista, CA, and introduced in 2010.

Echeveria affinis 'Black Prince'
'BLACK PRINCE' ECHEVERIA

▲ In a coppery pot, 'Black Prince' echeverias combine with a 'Sunburst' aeonium, 'Dragon's Blood' and coppertone stonecrops, red peperomia, and burgundy-flecked *Echeveria purpusorum* rosettes.

MATURE SIZE 4 to 6 inches wide
HARDINESS 20 degrees F

Succulents with reddish purple, burgundy, or yellow leaves, or with orange flowers combine beautifully with reddish brown *Echeveria affinis* 'Black Prince' and even darker, chocolate-hued *Echeveria affinis* 'Black Knight'. Dark leaves tend to show water spots; give the plants mineral-free (distilled) water or clean the leaves with the same.

Echeveria agavoides 'Lipstick'
LIPSTICK ECHEVERIA

Echeveria imbricata
BLUE ROSE

MATURE SIZE 4 to 6 inches wide
HARDINESS 20 degrees F

With its pointed leaves and crisp silhouette, this agave-like echeveria exhibits the edgier side of the genus. Glossy green leaves margined with crimson make lipstick echeveria as eye-catching as a chorus girl. Its offsets hug the main rosette tightly, adding to its appeal. The more sun the plant receives (short of burning), the more pronounced its red edges will be.

MATURE SIZE Rosettes to 8 inches in diameter
HARDINESS 20 degrees F

The symmetry of *Echeveria imbricata* is exquisite. Azure rosettes produce pups that hug the mother, forming overlapping circles. Plant one *Echeveria imbricata* rosette in the middle of a shallow, 18-inch-diameter pot, and in a year or so, offsets will have filled it. There's a reason this echeveria has been in cultivation longer than most: it's tough enough to grow in garden beds and handles full sun in all but desert climates.

Echeveria 'Perle von Nurnberg'
'PERLE VON NURNBERG' ECHEVERIA

MATURE SIZE 4 inches in diameter
HARDINESS 25 degrees F

'Perle von Nurnberg' echeverias are so perfectly symmetrical and pastel, they appear carved from soap. Of all the echeverias, they're among the most popular with florists. Combine the plants with creamy white roses in a wedding bouquet, place them in pink or lavender pots as gifts, use them in floral-style succulent compositions, but don't plant them in the open garden because their leaves are too easily marred.

▲ A floral-style arrangement combines a dozen different rosette succulents, including 'Perle von Nurnberg' echeveria (right).

Echeveria subrigida 'Fire and Ice'
'FIRE AND ICE' ECHEVERIA

MATURE SIZE 12 to 18 inches wide
HARDINESS 20 degrees F

This echeveria's wavy leaves have a painterly
wash of cool hues bordered with ribbons of red.
When bathed by late-afternoon sun, the plants
glow neon-bright. Despite its delicate appearance, 'Fire and Ice' does well in the garden, even
in nutrient-poor soils such as decomposed granite. Or display one in a pale blue or crimson pot.

Echinocactus grusonii
GOLDEN BARREL CACTUS

MATURE SIZE 3 feet in diameter over time
HARDINESS 15 degrees F

When I first saw these members of the genus *Echinocactus* (ee-KINE-oh-kak-tus) in a succulent landscape, I asked the owner why he had them. Weren't such prickly plants difficult to garden around? He had me stand so I could see the late afternoon sun behind them, and suddenly it made sense: their translucent spines are beautiful when backlit. Halo effect aside, these plants' yellow color, spherical shape, and fuzzy texture enhance any dry garden.Though becoming common in Southwest gardens, golden barrels are nearly extinct in the wild. In order to bloom, they need to attain 14 inches in diameter—which takes fourteen years of growth. Satiny yellow flowers, followed by seed capsules and brown tufts, form a corona around the top of the plant. Grow at least three for best effect and give them superb drainage; as with all cacti, golden barrels may rot if overwatered.

Echinocereus triglochidiatus
CLARET CUP CACTUS

MATURE SIZE 10 inches high
HARDINESS −20 degrees F

This diminutive cactus, a member of the genus *Echinocereus* (ee-ky-noh-SIR-ee-us), is massed with vivid, waxy flowers in spring. Buttercup-like blooms contrast with the plant's no-nonsense needles. Grow in coarse, sandy soil, keep on the dry side, and position where you—and hummingbirds—can enjoy the flowers. For a cheerful display, pair with a pot the same vermillion as the blooms.

◀ Golden barrel cactus
(*Echinocactus grusonii*) with
blue hens-and-chicks

Euphorbias

The genus *Euphorbia* (u-FOR-bee-ah) is immense and by no means limited to succulents—poinsettias, for example, are included. Succulent euphorbias may resemble cacti but are native to Africa rather than the desert Southwest and Mexico. Spines of cacti radiate from a central point (aureole), which euphorbias lack. Cactus flowers tend to be large and brilliantly hued; those of euphorbias are pealike spheres that open to tiny white or yellow blooms that are quite small relative to the plant. Take care: the milky sap of euphorbias is caustic and extremely irritating to the eyes. Should you get it on your skin, wash thoroughly with soap and water.

Don't plant euphorbias in areas where children and pets play.

Many euphorbias resemble coral and other undersea creatures. Among the look-alikes included here are medusoid euphorbias, fire sticks, Tanzanian zipper plant, 'Snowflake', and baseball plant. Others worth seeking for an undersea scene are the crested form of *Euphorbia lactea* (alabaster swirl), *Euphorbia resinifera* (resin spurge), and *Euphorbia leucodendron* (pencil cactus).

▼ Medusa's head euphorbia (*Euphorbia caput-medusae*)

Euphorbia, medusoid

MEDUSA-FORM EUPHORBIAS ◄

MATURE SIZE 18 inches in diameter
HARDINESS 23 degrees F

Medusoid (snakelike, named after Medusa in Greek mythology) euphorbias form pinwheels of cylindrical, scaly green leaves that radiate from a central point. Among the best known are *Euphorbia esculenta*, *Euphorbia inermis*, *Euphorbia woodii*, *Euphorbia flanaganii*, and appropriately named *Euphorbia caput-medusae*. Readily available *Euphorbia flanaganii* 'Cristata' (crested) looks very different from the species—like wavy green coral. Look down into a large medusoid euphorbia and you'll see what looks like the whorled center of a sunflower; it's another example of a Fibonacci spiral. Round containers and urns are perfect for showcasing these elegant yet edgy plants.

Euphorbia ammak 'Variegata'

AFRICAN CANDELABRA

MATURE SIZE 12 feet tall
HARDINESS 27 degrees F

I once visited a San Diego grower who had African candelabra trees by the dozens, all in the ground and all taller than I: a forest of euphorbias. Wavy edges give this prickly, columnar succulent a distinctive silhouette. Stems of the variegate are such a pale green, they're almost white. They are easy to start from cuttings, but watch out for the caustic sap. When truncated, the plant will branch upward at the cut end, creating a saguaro-like silhouette. Protect from overwatering and excessive rainfall (20+ inches a year) lest the trunk rot.

Similar in appearance to *Euphorbia ammak* is green-only *Euphorbia ingens*, which is less frost tolerant. Both, over time, become immense trees with multiple vertical branches. An unusual (and oft-photographed) variety of *Euphorbia ingens* is at Lotusland near Santa Barbara; its stems loop downward and snake along the ground.

Euphorbia anoplia
TANZANIAN ZIPPER PLANT

Euphorbia milii
CROWN OF THORNS

MATURE SIZE 1 to 3 feet tall and wide, depending on variety
HARDINESS 28 degrees F

MATURE SIZE 6 to 12 inches high
HARDINESS 25 degrees F

This diminutive, columnar euphorbia offsets to form dense clusters. Green-and-cream stripes along the multi-angled stem suggest a zipper. When seen from above, the faceted plants and their offsets are fat little green stars.

Don't be put off by crown of thorns' spiny branches. Rather, notice how they're tipped with sprays of dime-sized bracts (leaf clusters that look like flowers) that resemble, from a distance, geraniums. Bracts of this useful shrub—which is seldom out of bloom—come in all warm colors, including red, yellow, coral, and cream. Dwarf cultivars are ideal for potted arrangements and include those so floriferous that at first glance you'd think they were hydrangeas. One example is *Euphorbia milii* 'Dwarf Apache'; it has a compact growth habit and rose-red bracts.

Euphorbia obesa

OBESA, BASEBALL PLANT

MATURE SIZE 4 inches wide by 6 inches high
HARDINESS 28 degrees F

I call these chubby little succulents by their species name *obesa* because I prefer it to the more mundane "baseball plant." In 1925 obesas were so rare, one sold for $27.50 (an exorbitant amount, then, for a plant). Fortunately, the price has dropped significantly.

Obesas illustrate an important rule: the fatter and fleshier the succulent, the less water it requires and the more prone it is to rotting. I learned this the hard way when I left a potted obesa out in the rain; shortly thereafter, it turned squishy and collapsed. Its successor is an obesa that, as I discovered after I bought it, had no roots. It was fine for the several months it took to regenerate them; in fact, the stress of being rootless turned the plant from green to a pretty reddish brown. Obesas will elongate over time unless grown in perfectly bright and balanced light. In spring they sport topknots of beadlike blooms.

Euphorbia polygona 'Snowflake'
'SNOWFLAKE' EUPHORBIA

MATURE SIZE 6+ inches in diameter by 12 to 18 inches high
HARDINESS 25 degrees F

This cylindrical, deeply ribbed succulent forms tight hens-and-chicks colonies. If you're a spine lover, look for its cousin, *Euphorbia horrida*, which as the name suggests is so bristly it's scary. Both lend great texture and interest to dry gardens. Topdress with red volcanic rock, which contrasts with the plants and echoes the color of their buds. Position these euphorbias so that their rippled edges and carousel-like crowns can be seen and enjoyed.

▼ *Euphorbia horrida*

Euphorbia tirucalli 'Sticks on Fire'
FIRE STICKS

Faucaria tigrina
TIGER JAWS

MATURE SIZE Clusters to 6 or more inches wide
HARDINESS 32 degrees F

MATURE SIZE 6+ feet tall and as wide (when grown in the ground)
HARDINESS 32 degrees F

Euphorbia tirucalli 'Sticks on Fire' forms a thicket of loosely branching, vertical stems, each about the diameter of a chopstick (thicker over time) and lacking prominent leaves. Use the plant to lend color and height to container compositions, to add a vertical accent in water-wise gardens, to resemble an autumn-hued tree in miniature landscapes, and to suggest coral in succulent seascapes. Not all plants sold as fire sticks will turn brilliant colors; some may redden only at branch tips. Although fire sticks do become redder in winter and when stressed, expect the color to stay pretty much the same as when you bought it (unless it's grown in shade, which will turn it green).

At first glance, tiger jaws, a member of the genus *Faucaria* (foh-KAHR-ee-ah), looks like it might be a carnivorous plant. White, threadlike extensions from the margins of wedge-shaped leaves make them resemble snapping jaws. No worries, this succulent is all growl and no bite. It does well as a windowsill plant. Keep on the dry side, especially during summer dormancy, and provide plenty of light from late summer through midwinter to encourage bloom. In November, tiger jaws spits out shimmering yellow, ice-plant flowers that are large in proportion to the plant.

Furcraea foetida 'Mediopicta'
MAURITIUS HEMP

MATURE SIZE 6 feet tall and wide
HARDINESS 25 degrees F

Closely related to *Agave* is the genus *Furcraea* (fur-CRAY-ah), which includes lovely *Furcraea foetida* 'Mediopicta'. Although this fountain of upright and tapered green-and-yellow leaves is native to South America, it is best known for its cultivation on the African island of Mauritius as a source of hemp fiber. Unlike some agaves and other furcraeas, its leaves are not stiff or serrated, but their softness comes with a downside—the foliage is easily damaged. Protect from scorching sun, frost, wind, and leaf-chewing pests such as snails. Furcraeas are monocarpic and don't pup, but their inflorescences (bloom spikes) attain a majestic 30 to 40 feet tall, with thin branches lined with so many little plants, you'll be able to start a hemp business.

Gasteraloe 'Green Ice'
'GREEN ICE' GASTERALOE

MATURE SIZE 6 inches in diameter
HARDINESS 32 degrees F

Gasteraloes (gas-ter-AH-lohs) are hybrids that result from crossing aloes with gasterias. Of the half dozen or so available in specialty nurseries, one has become a superstar: 'Green Ice'. A cross of partridge breast aloe and *Gasteria* 'Little Warty', it has thick, pale green leaves striated with darker green. Despite its delicate color, 'Green Ice' does fine in full sun in all but desert climates. Combine it in a dish garden with its horticultural parents for an intriguing juxtaposition of shapes, colors, textures, and flowers.

Gasteria species
GASTERIAS

▲ Bicolor gasteria (*Gasteria bicolor*)

MATURE SIZE 6 to 24 inches wide, depending on variety
HARDINESS 32 degrees F

The genus name *Gasteria* (gas-TEER-ee-ah) comes from the plants' slender bloom spikes lined with what look like little pink stomachs. Gasterias have thick-skinned, stiff, unyielding leaves that are wedge- or tongue-shaped and that may be covered with raised dots. Bicolor gasteria's slender foliage starts out as a fan, then grows into an irregular rosette. *Gasteria bicolor* 'Liliputana' is a miniature version, as the name suggests. Aloes and gasterias are related, and larger gasterias suggest aloes with unusually thick leaves. Gasterias thrive in bright shade, but sun will help to redden those so inclined. The leaves are prone to snapping off, but a broken leaf inserted into the soil may yield new plants.

Graptopetalum paraguayense
GHOST PLANT

MATURE SIZE Rosettes to 4 inches in diameter, stems to 18 inches or longer
HARDINESS 15 degrees F

Graptopetalum (grap-toh-PET-ah-lum) rosettes resemble echeverias, to which they are related. Overlapping, rounded triangles of graptopetalum leaves form a Fibonacci spiral.

The common name ghost plant probably has to do with the look of the grayish white, opalescent leaves. These turn pinkish yellow in hot, dry conditions and blue-gray when pampered with partial shade and regular water. The plants come not from Paraguay, as the species name implies, but Mexico. Rosettes grow at the tips of ever-lengthening stems that become pendant over time, so graptopetalums make good cascaders. Handle with care; leaves of graptopetalums detach readily. Because fallen leaves can form new little plants and cuttings from ghost plants root effortlessly, these are among the easiest succulents to propagate.

Graptoveria 'Fred Ives'
'FRED IVES' GRAPTOVERIA

MATURE SIZE 8 inches in diameter
HARDINESS 28 degrees F

Graptoverias (grap-toh-VEH-ree-ahs) are bigeneric hybrids of echeverias and graptopetalums. Depending on the time of year, temperature, and sun exposure, rosettes of 'Fred Ives' graptoveria may blend shades of blue, teal, gray, rose, or yellow. I have them in the open garden, where they have breezed through frosty nights, searing summer sun, and benign neglect. I assumed my plants looked great until I compared them to graptoverias in a garden closer to the coast. *Graptoveria* 'Fred Ives' exhibits its appreciation of a mild maritime climate by growing even larger and more robust. And unlike succulents that have to be stressed to be more colorful, graptoverias turn deeper and richer hues under ideal conditions.

Graptoveria 'Opalina'
'OPALINA' GRAPTOVERIA

MATURE SIZE 6 inches in diameter
HARDINESS 28 degrees F

Less common than 'Fred Ives', 'Opalina' graptoveria has shorter, fatter leaves, and varies in color from pale silvery blue to pinkish lavender. As the name implies, these hues have a lovely opalescent sheen.

Haworthias

Enjoy haworthias (hah-WOR-thee-ahs), diminutive succulents from South Africa, in windowsill pots, miniature landscapes, terrariums, and dish gardens. These popular houseplants thrive in low-light conditions. They also are among the easiest succulents to crossbreed in order to create hybrids—a pursuit of avid collectors. As with any windowsill plant, take care not to let ultraviolet rays, magnified by windowpanes, burn haworthias. And should you move them outdoors in spring and summer, keep in mind that direct sun can scorch plants unaccustomed to it. Indoors, especially if air circulation is minimal, check leaf axils often for insect infestations. Spray or dab pests with diluted isopropyl alcohol.

▶ 'Snow White' zebra plant (*Haworthia attenuata* 'Snow White')

Haworthia attenuata
ZEBRA PLANT ◂◂

MATURE SIZE 5 inches high
HARDINESS 32 degrees F

Zebra plants (*Haworthia attenuata*) have stiff, pointed leaves that appear sharp but aren't. Parallel ridges composed of white dots give the plants texture, and contrast with the dark green of the leaves. As with most *Haworthia* species, this one has numerous cultivars, but one worth seeking in particular is 'Snow White'. Its leaves are so thickly ribbed with white, they suggest snow-covered conical trees. *Haworthia attenuata* often is mislabeled *Haworthia fasciata*, and indeed, they look almost the same. The latter, which is uncommon, has leaves that are smooth on the inside (upper) surface, while those of *Haworthia attenuata* are knobby on both sides (though to a lesser extent on the inside). Both share the common name zebra plant.

Haworthia limifolia
FAIRY WASHBOARD

▲ Variegated fairy washboard (*Haworthia limifolia* 'Variegata')

MATURE SIZE 2 inches high by 4 inches wide
HARDINESS 32 degrees F

Fairy washboard (*Haworthia limifolia*) has pointed and ridged leaves that you won't be able to resist touching. The solid green form can be found in most succulent specialty nurseries; the variegate is not as common. The look of the plant alone is enough to endear it to children, but if that doesn't do it, its fanciful name will.

Haworthia turgida
WINDOWPANE PLANT

MATURE SIZE 3 inches in diameter
HARDINESS 32 degrees F

Windowpane plant has pointed leaves, offsets readily, and is bright green. Areas of translucent tissue at leaf tips make them resemble green gelatin. Other haworthias that share this intriguing characteristic include *Haworthia cooperi*, *Haworthia cymbiformis*, *Haworthia truncata*, and *Haworthia retusa*.

Hesperaloe parviflora
RED HESPERALOE

MATURE SIZE 2½ feet tall (not including flowers)
HARDINESS 0 degrees F or lower

Tall hesperaloe (hes-per-AH-loh) bloom stalks will look you right in the eye. Flowers come in shades of yellow, red, and pink and are beautiful when mixed. Slender gray-green leaves are stiff but not spiky and form an upright, arching fountain. Threadlike white filaments peel away from leaf margins, add texture, and give the sun something to backlight. Red hesperaloe, which has succulent roots, is an outstanding plant for desert gardens. Once established it survives on rainfall alone but will give a better bloom show with twice-monthly summer water. If it has a downside, it's that deer find it delectable.

Hoya species
WAXFLOWER

MATURE SIZE Several feet or more in length
HARDINESS 40 degrees F

Hoyas (HOY-ahs) are succulent vines native to Thailand. Blooms, which appear in summer, consist of waxy, star-shaped flowers joined together like spokes of an umbrella to create a half-sphere. Although hoyas are grown primarily for their blooms, those with interesting foliage are worth seeking. Leaves of Hindu rope (*Hoya compacta*) are curled and intertwined, and suggest tortellini noodles. *Hoya kerrii* has heart-shaped leaves that make its blooms almost irrelevant. Many species of *Hoya* are variegated, too. Hoyas do best in temperatures above 50 degrees, in bright shade. Most can be cultivated indoors. The flower show is best when the plants are rootbound. Grow in regular potting soil blended with 30 percent orchid mix. Keep on the dry side, and grow in a hanging basket or train along a trellis.

ICE PLANTS ▶

MATURE SIZE 3 to 18 inches high, spreading to several feet or more
HARDINESS 20 degrees F and lower

Once lumped under the genus *Mesembryanthemum*, ice plants are still referred to as "mesembs" by horticulturists. Many of these plants are in the genus *Lampranthus*, a name that, to my consternation, seems continually in flux, changing to *Ruschia* or *Oscularia* and then back again. A few ice plants live up to the name and are quite cold tolerant, notably those belonging to the genus *Delosperma*. None tolerate foot traffic. Most mesembs blast forth with vivid-hued, shimmering, multipetaled blooms in spring.

Use ice plants as ground covers and lawn substitutes and combine them in containers, hanging baskets, window boxes, and terraces. Flowers open in sun and close in low light.

◀ Two different colors of ice plant create an eye-popping display.

▼ Ice plants can add color to dish gardens too.

Kalanchoes

Shapes and textures of kalanchoe (kah-lan-KOH-ee) leaves range from smooth, green, and glossy to nubby, gray, and jagged. Flowers vary from clusters of tiny stars to bean-sized bells on multibranched stalks. In habitat, the plants are found from South Africa to Vietnam, along the tropical latitudes of the world. They are relatively new to cultivation, having been introduced to the nursery trade during the latter half of the twentieth century. Kalanchoes are frost tender, but those with well-established roots may regenerate after the plant dies to the ground. Pronunciation of the genus seems to vary by region. If you prefer kah-LAN-cho, I don't mind.

▶ Paddle plant, backlit

Kalanchoe beharensis 'Fang'
FELT BUSH, VELVET LEAF

MATURE SIZE 2 to 3 feet tall
HARDINESS 25 degrees F

Kalanchoe beharensis 'Fang' is a succulent in
need of a shave. Its grizzled protuberances,
which somewhat resemble fangs, are fuzzy yet
stiff. Despite its eccentric appearance, 'Fang' is
as easy to grow as any succulent, either in pots
or in the ground. I have it in a square container
that emphasizes the leaves' angularity.

The species, *Kalanchoe beharensis* (Napoleon's hat), has leaves like stiff felt that are the
same gray as 'Fang' but lack its gnarled outcrop-
pings. In a frost-free garden, Napoleon's hat will
grow into a tree over time, attaining 6 feet or
more. Both it and 'Fang' do well in the garden
and in pots.

Kalanchoe blossfeldiana
SUPERMARKET KALANCHOE

MATURE SIZE 8 inches high
HARDINESS 32 degrees F

A widely sold and popular houseplant, *Kalanchoe blossfeldiana* has shiny, dark green leaves
with scalloped edges. It's grown primarily for its
flowers, and its many cultivars produce masses
of dainty blooms in assorted candy hues. I like
to mix colors that have the same intensity, such
as hot pink, bright orange, and school-bus yellow. Pastel varieties serve as pretty centerpieces
for bridal and baby showers. Blooms of some
cultivars combine several colors, such as coral,
golden yellow, and salmon pink. Calandivas are a
type of *Kalanchoe blossfeldiana* with multipetaled
flowers that resemble tiny cabbage roses.

In being bred for widespread distribution,
these succulents have also been bred for tough-
ness. Like commercial poinsettias, supermarket kalanchoes can take a lot of abuse. They'll
even bloom in low light, making them good for
indoor dish gardens. The plants flower every six
months or so and keep their blooms six weeks
or more, but this takes its toll; the plants become
leggy and need to be replaced. Take cuttings if
you want more of a certain color.

Kalanchoe luciae
PADDLE PLANT, FLAPJACK PLANT

▲ *Kalanchoe thyrsiflora* at the Huntington Botanical Gardens

▶ Paddle plant (*Kalanchoe luciae*)

MATURE SIZE 18 inches high
HARDINESS 28 degrees F

Some paddle plants have overlapping, disc-shaped leaves; others, leaves that are larger and undulating. The main rosette, weakened by flowering, may die. Cut back the flower spike and pinch out any new buds that form. Or, after the plant elongates into bloom, you can harvest the half dozen or so miniatures of the mother from along the stalk. Cultivate in full sun in all but hottest climates to keep the leaves bright red. A new variegate, 'Fantastic', has cream-colored streaks.

Kalanchoe luciae is often mislabeled *Kalanchoe thyrsiflora*, but they are two different plants. The flowers of *Kalanchoe thyrsiflora* are dark yellow (those of *Kalanchoe luciae* are cream colored), and its oval gray-green leaves emerge in pairs at right angles to older, larger sets of leaves. *Kalanchoe thyrsiflora* is a good-looking plant that deserves to be more widely available.

Kalanchoe tomentosa
PANDA PLANT

MATURE SIZE 8 to 12 inches high
HARDINESS 32 degrees F

Panda plant is a bouquet of plush rabbit ears—silver-felted, oval leaves with brown stitches. As with other fuzzy succulents, you can gently sweep spilled potting soil or dust from the foliage with a soft paintbrush. Plant in a terracotta or red-glazed pot to repeat the leaf margins' russet hue. The species, which is silvery blue-gray, and cultivar 'Chocolate Soldier', which is golden brown, are my go-to plants when designing a multiplant combo; they add great texture and one or the other fits any color scheme.

◀ Panda plant (*Kalanchoe tomentosa*)

▼ *Kalanchoe tomentosa* 'Chocolate Soldier' combines with 'Dragon's Blood' sedum and golden *Kalanchoe orgyalis*.

Lithops species
LIVING STONES

MATURE SIZE 2 inches high
HARDINESS 32 degrees F

Specimens of *Lithops* (LITH-ops, which always is plural) resemble small, rounded pebbles— a camouflage that protects the plants, in their native habitat, from grazing animals. Lithops are from South Africa, where they subsist on scant rainfall. They need infrequent watering, low humidity, protection from frost, and four to five hours of bright but not intense sun a day. Too little light causes lithops to elongate.

Leave lithops alone from summer or fall (whenever they bloom) through spring (when the old leaves are dry and papery). That means *no* winter water. Around November, after producing shimmering yellow or white ice-plant flowers, the plant body will open to produce a new pair of leaves. As these grow, they feed off and absorb the old leaves, which gradually shrivel. In late spring and summer, observe the plants and water only if wrinkles appear for several days. (Late afternoon stress wrinkles do not count.) Let water drench the roots and flow out of the bottom of the pot. Every two weeks is plenty. When in doubt, don't water; these are among the most drought-tolerant plants on earth.

Grow lithops in coarse, free-draining soil, in a pot deep enough (at least 6 inches) to accommodate their long taproots. I display them with rounded stones that have similarly mottled, earthy colors.

Lithops species are not the only kinds of "living stones." Other living stones or "pebble plants" include argyrodermas, conophytums, baby toes (*Fenestraria* species), and split rocks (*Pleiospilos* species). All are highly sensitive to overwatering.

Mammillaria species
MAMMILLARIAS

MATURE SIZE 1 to 6 inches in diameter
HARDINESS varies

Mammillaria (mam-uh-LAIR-ee-ah) is the largest and most widely collected genus of spherical cacti. The name is Latin for nipple, and the plants have in common pointed bumps beneath dense spines. Mammillarias eventually form colonies that sport tiaras of brilliant, dainty flowers in spring or summer. Clumps of larger varieties may spread to 3 feet. Combine an assortment in wide, shallow pots to savor the rotund plants' repetitions and variations. Pincushion cactus (*Mammillaria celsiana*) is among the most popular; its spines are white, its flowers a corona of pink stars. Ladyfinger cactus (*Mammillaria elongata*) often is seen crested, its cylindrical stems transformed into fuzzy, brainlike convolutions.

◀ An assortment of mammillarias

▼ Pincushion cactus (*Mammillaria celsiana*)

Opuntia species
PRICKLY PEAR CACTUS

MATURE SIZE varies
HARDINESS 20 degrees F or less

Opuntia (oh-POON-tee-ah) is a useful if intimidating genus of pad-forming cactus. *Opuntia ficus-indica* is the most common, and I owe it one of my earliest memories of spines, pain, and tears. Despite that unpromising start, I've since come to like opuntias—two kinds in particular. *Opuntia ficus-indica* 'Burbank Spineless' was developed by Luther Burbank as cattle feed. It grows upwards of 6 feet tall, with oblong pads. Cattle didn't take to it, perhaps because of the bitter taste or the fact that it isn't entirely spine-less. For an opuntia, it's fairly harmless, and like most, will survive on rainfall alone even in the arid Southwest. It serves as a good contrast in shape and size to other succulents in a dry garden and is an excellent perimeter plant for homes in wildfire-prone areas.

Opuntia violacea is one of the loveliest cacti—indeed, one of the loveliest succulents. It is cold hardy (to 0 degrees F) and ideal for desert gardens where it receives the sun and heat it needs to maintain its remarkable teal-magenta-lavender hues. Yellow flowers bloom briefly, then collapse, leaving behind cupped bases that—as with all opuntias—swell into egg-shaped fruit.

Othonna capensis
LITTLE PICKLES

MATURE SIZE 2 to 3 inches high, spreading to 12 inches
HARDINESS 32 degrees F

This member of the genus *Othonna* (oh-THON-ah) is gaining popularity, in part thanks to the late horticulturist Bill Teague of the San Diego Botanic Garden. In 2011, when Teague was commemorated by a county fair display created by members of the San Diego Horticultural Society, *Othonna capensis* was prominently featured. I then discovered that my experience was similar to that of others: Teague had dropped by with a handful of cuttings that didn't look like much.

"It's a great ground cover that blooms non-stop," he'd assured me, as I silently wondered if the plant would survive my garden's less-than-ideal (that is, non-botanic-garden) conditions. *Othonna capensis*—which despite having the common name little pickles, should be "the Bill Teague plant"—soon became a mainstay in my garden and others he introduced it to.

Similar to the succulent senecios it resembles, *Othonna capensis* likes warmth, regular water, bright light, and a dry rest in summer. When the plant is stressed, leaves turn shades of yellow, lavender, and red. Yellow, dime-sized, daisylike flowers top slender stems autumn through spring.

Pachycereus marginatus
MEXICAN FENCE POST

MATURE SIZE 20 feet tall
HARDINESS 25 degrees F

Mexican fence post, a member of the genus *Pachycereus* (pak-ee-SEER-ee-us), is native to central and southern Mexico, where it's planted in lines to demarcate property boundaries. Older plants branch from the base, eventually forming V-shaped clumps. If you want it to grow rapidly—up to 3 feet a year—alternate deep soakings with allowing the soil to go dry. Spines, though sharp, are short, so Mexican fence post is generally not a problem near pathways. In spring, thumb-size cream-colored flowers line the ribs. Reddish fruit the size of marbles follows. Solo plants look lonely, so whether or not you use it as a fence, grow it in multiples.

Pachypodium lamerei
MADAGASCAR PALM ▶

MATURE SIZE 10 feet tall over time
HARDINESS 25 degrees F

Madagascar palm, the most common species of *Pachypodium* (pak-ee-POH-dee-um) has silvery, prickly branches with topknots of bright green, lancelike leaves. The common name is a misnomer; though from Madagascar, this is not a palm at all. Pachypodiums do well in pots. Subspecies *inermis* is thornless with a trunk lined with green tubercles where leaves once were attached. It may take a young pachypodium four or more years before it blooms. Large, fragrant, saucer-shaped flowers are followed by ornamental seedpods that resemble horns. These are large and woody, with seeds attached to a fuzzy canopy. Once pachypodiums bloom, their trunks bifurcate (split into branches).

Withhold water during dormancy, midautumn through midspring. Water well when nighttime temperatures exceed 60 degrees, then begin to cut back. Plant on a slope, if possible, so water drains away from the roots. Take care not to damage or pierce the pachy (elephantine) parts of the plant, especially the base, when trimming or transplanting.

Pedilanthus bracteatus (Euphorbia bracteata)
SLIPPER PLANT

Peperomia graveolens 'Ruby'
RUBY PEPEROMIA

MATURE SIZE 4 to 8 feet tall, spreading 3 to 4 feet
HARDINESS 25 degrees F

Upright, slender, cylindrical stems make pedilanthus (ped-uh-LAN-thus) useful as a vertical element for large pots and garden beds. This Baja California native is effective solo or massed. In early summer light red bracts appear near the branch tips. The red flowers of *Pedilanthus* species resemble ladies' slippers—the Greek for shoe is *pedil* and for flower is *anthos*. Give full sun to light shade and minimal water; mature plants can get by on rainfall alone in southern California. Better-known *Pedilanthus macrocarpus* also has the common name slipper plant. It is leafless, smaller (to 4 feet tall), slower growing, and not as cold tolerant, and it has a messier silhouette—its stems curve and bend from their own weight.

MATURE SIZE 8 inches high
HARDINESS 40 degrees F

As recently as the 1990s ruby peperomia (pep-uh-ROH-mee-ah) was rare in cultivation, but since then its brilliant leaves have made it a player in the nursery marketplace. There's little information on how to care for it, but as with any plant, it helps to know where it comes from, and this jewel is native to Ecuadorian jungles. It likes warmth and humidity, and bright light but not full sun. Grow it as a potted succulent; this is not an in-ground plant unless you live in the tropics. Bloom spikes are slender pipe cleaners massed with yellowish white flowers so tiny they're nearly microscopic. Get close enough and you may detect an unpleasant odor; *graveolens* means bad smelling.

Portulacaria afra 'Variegata'
VARIEGATED ELEPHANT'S FOOD

◀ Variegated elephant's food
(*Portulacaria afra* 'Variegata')

▼ Variegated elephant's food
in a poolside urn

MATURE SIZE Trailing stems 12 to 18 inches long
HARDINESS 28 degrees F

Elephant's food is sometimes confused with *Crassula ovata* (jade plant) because they look alike, but portulacaria (pohr-choo-lah-KAIR-ee-ah) leaves are smaller and the stems wiry—in fact, the stems are difficult to sever without clippers or a knife (something you may discover, as I did, if you surreptitiously attempt to take a cutting). Portulacarias are tough and malleable, easily handle drastic pruning, and make good bonsai subjects. The species (*Portulacaria afra*) grows into an ungainly, multistemmed shrub 6 to 8 feet tall. Variegated elephant's food (*Portulacaria afra* 'Variegata') is a trailing plant with wine red stems lined with half-inch, oval, yellow-streaked leaves. It's excellent as a gap filler, cascader, mounding ground cover, or terrace filler. Also look for *Portulacaria afra* 'Minima', a flexible-stemmed, prostrate variety with slightly smaller, emerald leaves and red stems; it's great in pots and hanging baskets.

Rhipsalis species
RHIPSALIS, MISTLETOE CACTUS

MATURE SIZE Trailing to several feet
HARDINESS 40 degrees F

Members of the genus *Rhipsalis* (RHIP-sah-lis) are tree-dwelling (epiphytic) cacti from South America, mainly Brazil. The plants have branching, pendant stems that usually are cylindrical but may be flat or angled. Spines, if present, are fine and hairlike; flowers, tiny and white. Fruits that grow along the stems resemble gooseberries. The name comes from the Greek *rhips*, meaning "wickerwork." Grow as you would any tropical cacti (see *Schlumbergera*). Keep at room temperature throughout the year and reduce water in winter. Good for hanging baskets and vertical gardens indoors (with good air circulation) and low-light areas of the garden.

Sansevieria species
MOTHER-IN-LAW'S TONGUE, SNAKE PLANT ▶

MATURE SIZE 1 to 3 feet tall, depending on variety
HARDINESS 32 degrees F

Sansevierias (san-suh-VEHR-ee-ah) make excellent houseplants, as they tolerate dim light, require minimal water, and like the same temperatures humans do. With their vertical, tapered, and rigid leaves, the plants provide intriguing linear shapes and vertical interest to container compositions and shady garden beds. The simple silhouette of sansevierias lends elegance to any setting but is especially suited to contemporary interiors and architecture. Sansevierias are unfussy about soil. The key to keeping them healthy is to water regularly during warm months and not at all during cool. The plants spread via underground rhizomes that will crowd a pot to the point that it may crack and break. If roots are thickly massed, use a hacksaw to divide them. Do not place a sansevieria where a pet might chew it; the plants contain saponins that are toxic to dogs and cats.

◀ *Sansevieria trifasciata* 'Moonglow'

▼ *Sansevieria cylindrica*

◀ *Sansevieria trifasciata* 'Laurentii'

Schlumbergera and *Hatiora* hybrids
THANKSGIVING, CHRISTMAS, AND EASTER CACTUS

MATURE SIZE 12 inches high by 18 inches wide
HARDINESS 35 degrees F

Hatiora (HAH-tee-ohr-ah) hybrids, commonly called Easter cacti, bloom in April and May. Easter cacti are often confused with *Schlumbergera* (shlum-BEHR-juhr-ah) hybrids—known as Thanksgiving and Christmas cacti due to November or December flowering—because their leaves (which actually are flattened stems) are similar. However, flowers of spring bloomers are star-shaped; those of winter bloomers are elongated and have protruding stamens.

Keep these Brazilian beauties between 70 and 80 degrees F during the day and 55 to 65 degrees F at night. Grow in pots or hanging baskets in bright indirect light plus an hour or two of early morning or late afternoon sun. Water well but don't allow to become waterlogged. Three months before bloom time, when buds need to form, keep plants drier and cooler than usual (50 to 60 degrees F) and in total darkness at night.

▲ Christmas cactus (*Schlumbergera* hybrid)

▶ Easter cactus (*Hatiora* hybrid)

Sedums

Sedum (SEE-dum) is a large genus, and low-growing varieties do well in rock gardens, hence the common name stonecrop. Nurseries and garden centers sell ornamental sedums by the flat. Combine an assortment to make a patch-work garden, perhaps in a trough; to fill gaps between stepping stones; and as filler plants for dish gardens. In general, the smaller and finer the leaf, the more cold hardy the stonecrop and the less it likes hot sun. Leaves may root where they fall, or you can dig up a clump with a garden trowel and transplant it. Pinch back to encourage fullness. Stems usually branch from the cut end and you can replant the tips.

Sedums produce clusters of five-pointed yellow, pink, or white star-shaped flowers in spring.

Perennial shrub sedums (*Sedum spectabile*, *Sedum telephium*, and their hybrids) are drought tolerant, quite cold hardy (to −30), and grow in all but desert climates. The plants, which attain 1 to 2 feet in height, die to the ground in winter and then return from the roots in spring. They bloom from late summer through fall, make good cut flowers, and when dry add interest to the winter garden—especially when dusted with snow.

▼ Golden stonecrop (*Sedum makinoi* 'Ogon')

Sedum species, small
SMALL STONECROPS

MATURE SIZE 4 to 6 inches high, spreading 12 to 18 inches

HARDINESS 10 to −40 degrees F, depending on variety

Diminutive sedums are ideal for rockeries in cold climates where most other succulents won't survive outdoors. They have become popular for green roofs (verdant, ecologically sensible rooftop gardens). Small stonecrops also do well in vertical wall gardens, provided they get several hours of sun daily; otherwise, their stems will stretch toward light. Protect small sedums from heat in excess of 85 degrees F by keeping them out of full sun.

Angelina stonecrop (*Sedum* 'Angelina', to −40 degrees F) varies in color from chartreuse to yellow-orange, depending on how much sun it receives. Similar in form but different in hue is 'Blue Spruce' stonecrop (*Sedum* 'Blue Spruce', to −40 degrees F), with blue-gray foliage that suggests pine needles. Leaves of English stonecrop (*Sedum anglicum*, to −30 degrees F) resemble dark green grains of rice. *Sedum spathulifolium*, native to the western United States, includes silvery gray Cape Blanco stonecrop (*Sedum spathulifolium* 'Cape Blanco', to −30 degrees F) and lesser-known purple-hued 'Purpurium'. Both form tight clusters of dime-size rosettes. Those of 'Dragon's Blood' stone-

◀ 'Blue Spruce', 'Angelina', and 'Tricolor' stonecrops in a vertical garden

▲ 'Cape Blanco' stonecrop (*Sedum* 'Cape Blanco')

▼ 'Dragon's Blood' stonecrop (*Sedum* 'Dragon's Blood') repeats the shape and colors of red aeoniums.

◀◀ English stonecrop (*Sedum anglicum*) trails over the right side of a terracotta pot.

crop (*Sedum spurium* 'Dragon's Blood', to −40 degrees F) are red (with full sun) and scalloped. A mound of golden stonecrop (*Sedum makinoi* 'Ogon', to 0 degrees F) resembles buttered popcorn; it's a low-light succulent useful for brightening shady spots. With its cauliflower-like clusters of leaves and white forget-me-not flowers, Corsican stonecrop (*Sedum dasyphyllum*, to 10 degrees F) is a must for miniature gardens; October daphne (*Sedum sieboldii*, to −10 degrees F) has blue-gray leaves edged with red and maroon flowers in fall; and *Sedum pachyclados*, from Afghanistan (to −30 degrees F), has dime-size blue-green rosettes with toothed tips. There are numerous others.

Sedum species, warm-climate
MEXICAN STONECROPS

MATURE SIZE Stems 6 inches to 3 feet long, depending on variety
HARDINESS 28 degrees F or less, depending on species

Mexico is home to more than a hundred species of sedum. Perhaps the best known is burro tail (*Sedum burrito*), which is especially suited to hanging baskets because of its ever-lengthening stems massed with beadlike leaves. These are bluish green, do not fall off as readily as those of very similar donkey tail (*Sedum morganianum*), and grow in tightly clustered spirals. Burro tail is widely available in nurseries, but donkey tail is a pass-along plant, seldom for sale. The reason is that burro tail tolerates handling better than donkey tail, and stems denuded of leaves diminish a plant's commercial appeal. But donkey tail—which is a paler green—has been in cultivation longer, so it's as common as burro tail in gardens, if not more so.

The coppertone stonecrops (*Sedum nussbaumerianum* and *Sedum adolphii,* which some say are one and the same—in any case, the two are easily confused) have pointed leaves nearly 2 inches long at maturity. Plants are yellow-green in partial shade. Full sun turns the foliage a rosy gold that contrasts beautifully with lavender,

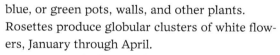
◀ *Sedum palmeri*

▲ Coppertone stonecrop (*Sedum nussbaumerianum*)

▼ *Sedum rubrotinctum* 'Pork and Beans' with a diminutive cultivar behind it, plus 'Angelina' sedum, and for height *Euphorbia leucodendron*

◀◀ Burro tail (*Sedum burrito*), left; *Sedum morganianum* (donkey tail), right

blue, or green pots, walls, and other plants. Rosettes produce globular clusters of white flowers, January through April.

Because the leaves of *Sedum rubrotinctum* are the size and shape of jelly beans, children invariably find them intriguing. The cultivar 'Pork and Beans' is a bright green that turns orange-red in full sun; cultivar 'Aurora' is a pastel blue-green that blushes pink.

Mexican bush sedum (*Sedum praeltum*), *Sedum kimnachii*, *Sedum confusum*, *Sedum palmeri* (often confused with similar *Sedum dendroideum*), and *Sedum mexicanum* have bright green leaves and are stellar performers in low-water, mild-climate gardens.

Sempervivum species
HOUSELEEKS, HENS-AND-CHICKS

MATURE SIZE Rosettes to 4 inches in diameter, spreading 12 inches or more, depending on variety

HARDINESS −10 degrees F (if dry)

Sempervivum (sem-per-VEE-vum) means always living, doubtless an acknowledgment of the plants' ability to tolerate cold, sun, and drought. The Harry Potterish common name, houseleek, originated in England, where the plants occasionally grow on roofs. Tight balls of leaves with pointed tips eventually multiply into clumps that may attain several feet in diameter. In strawberry jars and other containers, sempervivums will bubble over the edges and hug the sides. The genus comprises approximately forty species and more than three thousand cultivars. Native to the mountains of Europe, semps prefer a cool, dry location with perfect drainage. Plant in rock garden crevices or use to create carpets of texture and color in the garden. Keep them on the dry side in summer, when they are most at risk of rot from overwatering, and protect from temperatures above 75 degrees F. Most species can grow outdoors year-round in zones 4 through 7. In hotter regions, they are best cultivated in patio pots, in partial sun to bright shade. Star-shaped, rose-colored flowers open in the summer months. Rosettes die after flowering, but new ones quickly take their place.

A close relative of *Sempervivum* is *Jovibarba*, a genus of alpine succulents that are hardy to −10 or −20 degrees F. They look a lot like semps but reproduce differently. Offsets of *Jovibarba heuffelii* are squashed within the main rosette. Those of other members of this small genus are rollers, meaning they grow atop the mother plant and tumble off.

▶ Cobweb houseleek
(*Sempervivum arachnoideum*)
and a *Sempervivum* hybrid
(foreground)

◀◀ Roof houseleek
(*Sempervivum calcareum*)

Senecio

Senecio (suh-NEE-see-oh) is an immense genus in the daisy family, but succulent senecios are few, and of those, a mere handful are widely cultivated. Senecios are grown for the shape and color of their leaves and not for their blooms, which dry into dandelion-like tufts. These make the plant untidy, so I snip them off.

Blue senecio (*Senecio mandraliscae*) is a star performer, a versatile, readily available succulent that provides as much blue as a designer could possibly ask for, in the ground or in containers. Others listed here are mainly container plants, wonderful in hanging baskets. A shrub senecio also worth mentioning is most com-monly called *Senecio vitalis*, but experts sigh at this (I sympathize) and say it's *Senecio talinoides* ssp. *talinoides*, or *Senecio cylindricus*. Regardless, it's a terrific upright plant with slender, bright green leaves.

The hardiness of senecios, which are summer-dormant winter growers, varies by species; the blue senecios in my garden showed no damage when temperatures dropped to the mid-20s F. In summer, water only during the cool part of the day; heat-stressed senecios may rot if overwatered.

▼ Blue senecio (*Senecio mandraliscae*)

Senecio kleiniiformis
SPEAR HEAD

MATURE SIZE Stems to a foot or more in length
HARDINESS 20 degrees F

Leaves start out narrow and flare into slender, channeled fleurs-de-lis that form a starburst around the stem. The plant's airy appearance and trailing growth habit make it excellent for hanging baskets. The species is variable; in some instances, leaves may be shorter and spoon shaped. Plants become rangy over time; pinch back to encourage fullness.

Senecio mandraliscae (*Kleinia mandraliscae, Senecio talinoides* var. *mandraliscae*)
BLUE SENECIO ◄◄

MATURE SIZE 6 to 8 inches high
HARDINESS 20 degrees F

Blue senecio stays sky blue regardless of growing conditions. It's lovely planted in drifts and once established provides a source of cuttings to give away or to fill gaps in the garden. Use this creeping succulent to repeat the blue of agaves and to contrast with anything orange, from terracotta pots to California poppies. It also pairs beautifully with red-leaved aloes, lavender 'Afterglow' echeverias, fire sticks (*Euphorbia tirucalli* 'Sticks on Fire'), elephant's food (*Portulacaria afra* 'Variegata'), and burgundy-leaved 'Zwartkop' aeonium; and with nonsucculent companion plants such as ivy geranium, parrot's beak, and African daisies (*Gazania* species). Cut back in late summer. Because old leaves fall off and new ones grow at the ends of the stems, *Senecio mandraliscae* becomes lanky unless made to branch.

Similar in appearance but not as common is *Senecio serpens*, which is a better choice, if you can find it, for small beds and containers. Leaves are less than half the length of those of *Senecio mandraliscae*.

Senecio radicans 'Fish Hooks'
'FISH HOOKS' SENECIO, STRING OF BANANAS

▲ 'Fish Hooks' senecio (*Senecio radicans* 'Fish Hooks') with 'Perle von Nurnberg' echeverias

MATURE SIZE Stems several feet long
HARDINESS 32 degrees F

'Fish Hooks' senecio forms a waterfall of slender, flexible stems lined with canoe-shaped blue-green leaves. A pot atop a pedestal or a hanging basket serves as a perfect home for this trouble-free succulent that tolerates full sun in all but the hottest climates. It's a good design stand-in for more finicky string of pearls (*Senecio rowleyanus*).

Senecio rowleyanus
STRING OF PEARLS

MATURE SIZE 18 inches or longer
HARDINESS 32 degrees F

With pealike leaves on threadlike stems, string of pearls suggests dripping water, especially when planted in a dry fountain or birdbath. It's also useful for adding texture and a cascading element to hanging baskets and indoor arrangements. The plant prefers dappled shade and temperatures between 50 and 80 degrees F, and thus can be challenging to grow in any but mild coastal areas.

▶ String of pearls with 'Kiwi' aeonium and sedums

◀ String of pearls (*Senecio rowleyanus*) and echeverias

Trichocereus grandiflorus 'Red Star'
(*Echinopsis huascha*)

RED STAR CACTUS

MATURE SIZE 2½ feet tall
HARDINESS 15 degrees F

This columnar cactus, a member of the genus *Trichocereus* (tri-koh-SIR-ree-us), briefly blazes with blooms in warm hues that put on quite a show for pollinators. The fragile water lily–like flowers have a translucent, reflective sheen. When the plants are out of bloom, their polka-dotted ribs are their most engaging aspect. For an even more eye-catching display, combine with varieties that have yellow, cream, or orange flowers. A must for in-ground cactus gardens.

Yuccas

Ranging in habitat from Guatemala to Canada, yuccas (YUK-ahs) are unfussy succulents that thrive when pampered. Plant in a full-sun location in soil that drains well and give occasional deep soakings. Frequent watering produces faster growth; little to no water slows it. Most species tolerate temperatures below freezing. Several times a year, trim dry, downward-pointing leaves within a few inches of the trunk if you want a more tidy-looking tree. Protect yuccas from gophers, which not only eat the roots but also tunnel up the trunk.

Once established, yuccas can be difficult to remove. The base of the trunk expands into a bulbous mass that can break irrigation pipes, push against a home's foundation, and crack retaining walls. Those stiff, pointed leaves are treacherous, efficient at keeping predators and gardeners at bay. And yuccas, though slow growing, can get immense over time. Know a yucca's size at maturity and select its location wisely. Don't plant yuccas alongside walkways, or where children or pets might run into them.

Position yuccas where their leaves will be in silhouette, such as against the sky, a rock wall, or a boulder. Variegated yuccas with yellow-and-green striped leaves are especially beautiful backlit by early morning or late afternoon sun.

In addition to my two favorites shown here, Spanish bayonet and beaked yucca, other *Yucca* species that stand out include banana yucca (*Yucca baccata*, to 3 feet tall and 5 feet wide) which has leaves with sharp fibers along the edges; it may be stemless or have multiple short stems. Soaptree yucca (*Yucca elata*, to 20 feet tall over time) produces leaf clusters that look like green pincushions atop shaggy trunks. Adam's needle (*Yucca filamentosa*, to 5 feet tall and wide) resembles a narrow-leaved agave but has softer foliage. Spanish dagger (*Yucca gloriosa*, to 10 feet tall, 8 feet wide) is similar in appearance to *Yucca aloifolia* but forms multiple trunks. *Yucca recurvifolia* (to 10 feet tall and 8 feet wide) has a single trunk and soft, downward-curving blue-gray leaves; it spreads over time to create clumps. Our Lord's candle (*Yucca whipplei*, to 6 feet in diameter) is a rounded pincushion with toothed edges and sharp tips. *Yucca schidigera* (to 12 feet tall, 3 feet wide) is a bushy tree with daggerlike leaves.

Yucca aloifolia
SPANISH BAYONET

MATURE SIZE 8 feet tall or more
HARDINESS 0 degrees F

Spanish bayonet (*Yucca aloifolia*) has a slender trunk topped with swordlike leaves. In spring and summer, it produces plumes of cream-colored bells. One of the few succulents that thrives in sand and does not mind salt spray, this yucca grows well in beachfront gardens.

Spanish bayonet trees grow in a garden near my home and the owner lets me take cuttings, so I have added them to my own garden, positioning them where I needed a screen or to fill gaps. The branches are so lightweight, I can lift a 4-inch-diameter, 3-foot-long one with one hand. Using a serrated knife, I saw a limb off an existing tree, then bury the cut end. The hole needs only to be deep enough to hold the cutting upright, but root formation will be faster if the cutting is planted deeper. In any case, voilà: instant tree.

Yucca rostrata
BEAKED YUCCA ▶

MATURE SIZE 12 feet tall
HARDINESS 5 degrees F

Beaked yucca (*Yucca rostrata*) starts out spherical and then forms a trunk crowned with a shimmering topknot of slender leaves. It looks lovely in the landscape planted in multiples and also is attractive in pots. The origin of the common name beaked yucca is unclear but likely has to do with the flowers or fruit. Another common name, Nordstrom's yucca, originated when the plants were installed as decorations outside the department stores.

◀ Spanish bayonet (*Yucca aloifolia*) and gazanias

SUGGESTIONS FOR FURTHER READING

Baldwin, Debra Lee. 2007. *Designing with Succulents*. Portland, OR: Timber Press.

———. 2010. *Succulent Container Gardens*. Portland, OR: Timber Press.

Calhoun, Scott. 2012. *The Gardener's Guide to Cactus*. Portland, OR: Timber Press.

Chance, Leo. 2012. *Cacti and Succulents for Cold Climates*. Portland, OR: Timber Press.

Dortort, Fred. 2011. *The Timber Press Guide to Succulent Plants of the World*. Portland, OR: Timber Press.

Editors of Sunset Magazine. 2012. *The New Sunset Western Garden Book*, 9th ed. Birmingham, AL: Oxmoor House.

Irish, Mary, and Gary Irish. 2000. *Agaves, Yuccas and Related Plants: A Gardener's Guide*. Portland, OR: Timber Press.

Kelaidis, Gwen Moore. 2008. *Hardy Succulents*. North Adams, MA: Storey Publishing.

Morrison, Susan, and Rebecca Sweet. 2011. *Garden Up! Smart Vertical Gardening for Small and Large Spaces*. Minneapolis, MN: Cool Springs Press.

Pilbeam, John. 2008. *The Genus Echeveria*. British Cactus and Succulent Society.

Richardson, Fern. 2012. *Small-Space Container Gardens*. Portland, OR: Timber Press.

Schulz, Lorraine, and Attila Kapitany. 2005. *Echeveria Cultivars*. Teesdale, Victoria, Australia: Schulz Publishing.

Starr, Greg. 2012. *Agaves: Living Sculptures for Landscapes and Containers*. Portland, OR: Timber Press.

METRIC CONVERSIONS AND PLANT HARDINESS ZONES

INCHES / CENTIMETERS		FEET / METERS	
¼	0.6	¼	0.08
⅓	0.8	⅓	0.1
½	1.25	½	0.15
1	2.5	1	0.3
2	5.0	2	0.6
3	7.5	3	0.9
4	10	4	1.2
5	12.5	5	1.5
6	15	6	1.8
7	18	7	2.1
8	20	8	2.4
9	23	9	2.7
10	25	10	3.0

TEMPERATURES

$$°C = 5/9 \times (°F - 32)$$
$$°F = (9/5 \times °C) + 32$$

PLANT HARDINESS DATA FOR THE UNITED STATES

http://plianthardiness.ars.usda.gov/PHZMWeb/

PLANT HARDINESS DATA FOR CANADA

http://www.planthardiness.gc.ca/
or
http://atlas.nrcan.gc.ca/site/english/maps/environment/forest/forestcanada/planthardi

CREDITS

PHOTOS

Emma Alpaugh, 169

David Cristiani, The Quercus Group, Albuquerque, NM, 49

Marialuisa Kaprielian, Succulently Urban, San Diego, 57 right, 174 right

Marci Hunt LeBrun, 116, 118–123, 126–127, 130–134 above, 135, 141–142, 144–148, 150–154, 162–165, 168

Cristin Bisbee Priest, Simplified Bee, 81

Genevieve Schmidt, 21

Cate Schotl and Kristi Collyer, Green Thumb Garage, Laguna Niguel, CA, 109 lower right

Joe Stead, 22

Kit Wertz and Casey Schwartz of FlowerDuet, Los Angeles, 209

David Winger, 41 lower right

All other photographs are by Debra Lee Baldwin.

DESIGN

Akana Design, San Diego, 175 right

Emma Alpaugh, 130 above, 133 above, 135

Patrick Anderson garden, Fallbrook, CA, 87 right, 184 left, 254 left

Gary Bartl, Gardens by Gary Bartl, San Rafael, CA, 99 below

Sydney Baumgartner for Alice Van de Water, Santa Barbara, CA, 39 upper left

Jim Bishop garden, San Diego, 17 upper left, 180 right, 224 left, 232 right

Charlene Bonney, Encinitas, CA, 92 upper left

Linda Bresler for Elisabeth and Bo Matthys, Poway, CA, 2

Mary Brumbaugh, 181 left

Michael Buckner, The Plant Man nursery, San Diego, 35 upper left

Michael Buckner for Tina Back, San Diego, 94 right–95

Michael Buckner for Angela D'Amico and Dale Barbour, La Jolla, CA, 42

Michael Buckner for Bob and Judy Gennet, El Cajon, CA, 243 lower left

Michael Buckner for Chris and Robert Moore, La Jolla, CA, 195

Michael Buckner for Martin and Cynthia Offenhauer, San Diego, 38 right

Michael Buckner for Carolyn and Herb Schaer, Rancho Santa Fe, CA, 108 upper left, 199, 208 left

Michael Buckner for Lila Yee, San Diego, 86 upper right, 172

Brandon Bullard, Desert Theater Nursery, Escondido, CA, 31 lower left, 202 right, 224 right

California Cactus Center, 86 below, 94 left, 99 above, 109 upper right, 222 right

Chicweed, Solana Beach, CA, 25 above, 213 right

Cordova Gardens nursery, Encinitas, CA, 78, 197

Petra Crist, Rare Succulents Nursery, Rainbow, CA, 216

Elisabeth Crouch garden, Escondido, CA, 66 left, 180 left

Davis Dalbok, Living Green, San Francisco, 81

DIG Nursery, Santa Cruz, CA, 110 right

Kathy Doran, 92 lower right

Linda Estrin, 116, 124, 127, 128–129

Laura Eubanks, 107 left, 150, 153–155

Exquisite Orchids and Succulents, Torrance, CA, 44 above

Robyn Foreman, 93 above, 118, 121–123, 162, 165, 167, 168, 169, 247 lower right

Good Earth Nursery, Bonsall, CA, 188 left

Larry Grammer, 113 lower left

Bonnie Haman, 211 right

Pat Hammer, topiary for the San Diego Botanic Garden, 107 right

Jon Hawley, Chicweed, 138, 142–143

Huntington Botanical Gardens, San Marino, CA, 220 right

Peter and Margaret Jones garden, Escondido, CA, 87 left

Marialuisa Kaprielian, Succulently Urban, San Diego, 57 right, 174 right

Randy Laurie, Laurie's Landscaping, San Diego, 26 and 85 (with Frank Mitzel, Aesthetic Design)

David LeRoy and homeowner Stephanie Mills, 27

Matthew Maggio for Sherman Gardens, Corona del Mar, CA, 100–101, 104–105

Kathy McCarthy, Del Mar, CA, 203, 206

Jeanne and Barry Meadow garden, Fallbrook, CA, 82 left, 97

Patt Miller garden, San Diego, 43 above

Danielle Moher, 10

Jeff Moore, Solana Succulents, Solana Beach, CA, for the San Diego Botanic Garden, 109 lower left

Bill Munkacsy, Planta Seca, 113 right

Susan and Robert Munn garden, Davis, CA, 109 upper left

Felix Navarro, The Juicy Leaf, Venice, CA, 243 right

Hanh Nguyen, Bradbury, CA, 82 right

Monica Nochisaki garden, San Diego, 241 right, 248

Oasis Water Efficient Gardens, Escondido, CA, 37, 229 below

Frank and Susan Oddo garden, Elfin Forest, CA, 39 below, 251

Joseph Pagano, San Diego, 106

Tiffany Polli garden, Marina, CA, 28 above

Rancho La Puerta fitness spa, Baja California, 194

Rancho Soledad Nursery, Rancho Santa Fe, CA, 67

Mary Rodriguez garden, Rancho Santa Fe, CA, 84 below

Roger's Gardens nursery, Corona del Mar, CA, 17 upper right

Danielle Romero, Succulent Designs, Montebello, CA, 98

Michael Romero, Succulent Designs, Montebello, CA, 90, 108 lower left, 223 left

San Diego Botanic Garden, 86 upper left, 102 above, 107

Debbie Schaefer, clay mask for the San Diego Botanic Garden, 107 right

Suzy Schaefer garden, Rancho Santa Fe, CA, 41 above, 237

Christina Schiffman, 249 lower right

Cate Schotl and Kristi Collyer, Green Thumb Garage, Laguna Niguel, CA, 109 lower right

Seaside Gardens nursery, Carpinteria, CA, 108 right, 191 left, 254 right

Seasons Landscape, Laguna Beach, CA, 247 left

Kathy Short and Patti Canoles garden, Modesto, CA, 69 above

Patty Sliney, 92 upper right, 233 right

South Coast Botanic Garden, Palos Verdes Peninsula, CA, 182 right

Joe Stead for Anton and Jennifer Segerstrom, Corona del Mar, CA, 22, 192 right

Robin Stockwell, Succulent Gardens, Castroville, CA, 246

Jill Sullivan for the Nissen-Magiliato garden, Pacific Palisades, CA, 33

Eric and Stephanie Swadell garden, Escondido, CA, 207 right

Rebecca Sweet, Harmony in the Garden, Los Altos, CA, 110 left

Melissa Teisl, Chicweed, 144, 147–149

Terra Sol Garden Center, Santa Barbara, CA, 225

Tohono Chul Park, Tucson, AZ, 238

Char Vert, Pasadena, CA, 243 upper left

Waterwise Botanicals nursery, Escondido, CA, 89, 103, 201, 215 left

Kit Wertz and Casey Schwartz of FlowerDuet, Los Angeles, 209

Nick Wilkinson, Grow nursery, Cambria, CA, for Leslie and Kim Eady, Cayucos, CA, 25 right

INDEX

A

Acacia baileyana (Bailey's acacia), 50, 103

Adam's needle (Yucca filamentosa), 257

Aeonium arboreum 'Zwartkop' (black aeonium), 28, 90, 175, 253

Aeonium canariense (Canary Island aeonium), 16, 175

Aeonium 'Kiwi', 72, 91, 106, 129, 133, 147, 153, 176, 255

Aeonium nobile, 92

Aeonium species (aeoniums), 140
easy-care, 174–176
foliage, 93, 117

Aeonium 'Sunburst', 43, 84, 93, 176

African daisies (Gazania species), 103, 104, 253

'Afterglow' echeveria, 70–71, 104–105, 253

Agave americana (century plant), 16, 178

Agave americana 'Marginata' (striped century plant), 58, 86, 178

Agave americana 'Mediopicta Alba' (tuxedo agave), 23, 178, 188

Agave attenuata (fox tail agave), 60, 66, 140, 178–179

Agave attenuata 'Kara's Stripes', 26, 179

Agave bracteosa 'Green Spider', 180

Agave bracteosa 'Monterrey Frost', 180

Agave 'Cream Spike', 181

Agave desmettiana, 64–65

Agave desmettiana 'Variegata', 84, 174

Agave filifera, 99

Agave franzosinii, 60

Agave geminiflora, 206

Agave lophantha 'Quadricolor', 90, 129, 181

Agave parryi, 85, 182

Agave potatorum 'Kissho Kan' (butterfly agave), 182

agaves
blooming, 65–67
as deterrents to burglaries, 45
easy-care, 177–184
propagating, 58–61
rainbow foliage of, 23, 24, 26–27
succulent color wheel position of, 83
Taliesin West landscaped with, 17
temperature range for, 49

Agave shawii (Shaw's agave), 183

agave snout-nosed weevil, 75, 76

Agave utahensis (Utah agave), 183

Agave victoriae-reginae (Queen Victoria agave), 49, 184

Aleene's glue, 153

Alluaudia procera (Madagascan ocotillo), 184

Aloe, dwarf cultivars, 186

Aloe arborescens (torch aloe), 44, 45, 187

Aloe bainesii, 191

Aloe 'Blizzard', 187

Aloe 'Blue Elf', 188

Aloe brevifolia (short-leaf aloe), 147, 188

Aloe cameronii, 87, 90

Aloe ciliaris 'Firewall', 45

Aloe dichotoma, 191

Aloe 'Diego', 187

Aloe 'Doran Black', 141, 187

Aloe dorotheae (sunset aloe), 17, 90, 189

Aloe 'Fang', 187

Aloe ferox (Cape aloe), 189

Aloe harlana, 190

Aloe hemmingii (mosaic aloe), 98–99, 186, 190

Aloe 'Hercules', 191

Aloe humilis (spider aloe), 191

Aloe 'Lizard Lips', 141, 187

Aloe marlothii, 29

aloe mites, 74, 75, 76

Aloe nobilis (gold tooth aloe), 90, 129, 140, 188, 192

Aloe nobilis 'Variegata', 141

Aloe 'Pink Blush', 129, 187

Aloe plicatilis (fan aloe), 99, 192

Aloe polyphylla (spiral aloe), 193

aloes
diseases affecting, 75
easy-care, 185–186, 187–197
greenhouse, 52
mites attacking, 74
propagating, 60
succulent color wheel position of, 83

Aloe speciosa (tilt-head aloe), 193

Aloe striata (coral aloe), 194

Aloe vanbalenii (Van Balen's aloe), 32, 54, 194–195

Aloe variegata (partridge breast aloe, tiger aloe), 196–197

Aloe vera, 18, 38

Alpaugh, Emma, 131

Altman Plants (Vista, CA), 210

Anderson, Patrick, 9

'Angelina' stonecrop (Sedum 'Angelina'), 25, 37, 43, 90, 91, 129, 147, 148, 153, 246, 247, 249

Anigozanthos hybrids (kangaroo paw), 103, 104

antique cast-iron dollhouse bathtub, 108

aphids, 73, 76

Aporocactus flagelliformis (rat-tail cactus), 148, 197

Argyroderma patens, 35

argyrodermas ("living stones"), 234

Arizona-Sonora Desert Museum, 51

Artemisia 'Powis Castle' ('Powis Castle' wormwood), 90, 103

artichoke agave (Agave parryi var. truncata), 23